365
MEATLESS
MAIN DISH
MEALS

Other Books by William I. Kaufman

CHAMPAGNE
ART OF CASSEROLE COOKERY
ART OF CREOLE COOKERY
ART OF INDIA'S COOKERY
SUGAR FREE COOKBOOK
APPETIZERS & CANAPÉS COOKBOOK
FISH & SHELLFISH COOKBOOK
COFFEE COOKBOOK
PANCAKES, CREPES & WAFFLES COOKBOOK
NEW CAN OPENER COOKBOOK
WONDERFUL WORLD OF COOKING SERIES—4 VOLUMES
COOKING IN A CASTLE
GOURMET CHAFING DISH COOKBOOK
GOURMET BLENDER COOKBOOK
GOURMET FONDUE COOKBOOK
GOURMET BLENDER COOKBOOK
APPLE COOKBOOK
PLAIN AND FANCY CHICKEN COOKBOOK
PLAIN AND FANCY HAMBURGER COOKBOOK
PLAIN AND FANCY COOKIE COOKBOOK
NEW BLENDER COOKBOOK
UNICEF CHILDRENS BOOKS* SONGS, PRAYERS* POEMS*
LEGENDS

365
Meatless
Main Dish
Meals

———◆———

WILLIAM I. KAUFMAN

Doubleday & Company, Inc.
Garden City, New York
1974

Library of Congress Cataloging in Publication Data

Kaufman, William Irving, 1922–
365 meatless main dish meals.

1. Cookery. 2. Vegetarianism. I. Title.
TX837.K26   641.5
ISBN 0-385-01832-0
Library of Congress Catalog Card Number 73–10808

CONTENTS

INTRODUCTION

365 MEATLESS MAIN DISH MEALS is such an obvious title that I am not going to dwell too long on an explanation of what this book is about.

This volume has been written out of my deep distress over the steady augmentation of meat prices, to the point where I am contemplating swapping old gold pieces by weight in exchange for an equal amount of meat—a food that I have always considered essential to the well-being, to say nothing of the morale, of my family.

Another disturbing note has been introduced by the problem of planning meals that give proper nutrition in the absence of meat, without cutting down on over-all health. This book is proof that this problem is solvable.

Many of my readers have heard me say, "I write for the woman who cooks twenty meals per week for her family and one meal a week for her friends." This cookbook is for that woman. If you are looking for a zingy new way to prepare "Mousseline d'Écrevisses" or desire to create a sensation with my recipe for "Crêpes Soufflé," this is not the book for you. I suggest you consult others from among my eighty additional cookbooks as a source of this information.

In my home, although birth certificates indicate that we have only two children, my wife and I often have the impression we are running an old-fashioned stagecoach depot. For years we have been unable actually to sit down at the "family table" in the sense that everyone around the groaning board possesses the same family name. It is a family only because all of us, both young and old, share a common spirit of enjoying good conversation, exciting ideas, and love of delicious food. *Delicious food can be meatless.*

365 MEATLESS MAIN DISH MEALS is a very simple cookbook and does not require your having to devote many hours to meal preparation. In fact, if you fall into my favorite category (women who do things for others as well as for the family), you are probably so busy between home and outside activities that this volume will be a heaven-sent gift that permits you to whip up a quick repast only minutes after you have hit the door.

A few hints that will enhance your use of this book:

> Do not plan your main dish meals for the week unless you sit down with the local paper on the day all the supermarket sales are advertised

> Take a colored crayon and check every item that is a truly good bargain

> Go back once more through your list and circle main dish meal items that are on sale

You will then be ready to open this book to sections that relate to circled main dish meal items that are economical in price at your favorite shopping area. Your planning can extend over periods longer than a week if you can make good buys in things that are normally very costly. Let me explain.

Because I write cookbooks and lecture on cuisine and entertaining, I have to stay on top of modern developments and new ideas in food products. For this reason I shop regularly in at least two out of a selection of eight supermarkets in my neighborhood to keep abreast of marketing conditions. I often go to a special market for a particular sale to stock up on a featured item. If there are good purchases to be made of tuna, flounder, and Cheddar cheese all during the same week, I buy as great an amount as my budget will allow. I place the tuna on the storage shelves; the flounder I wrap, mark, and freeze; the Cheddar will be used for sandwiches and, depending on how much I buy, I will grate some and fill jars so the cheese will be readily available for future use in sauces, with pasta, or as topping for vegetables.

Great variety of tastes can be achieved by astute selection of recipes in this book, and, if your budget will not stretch long or wide enough for extensive entertaining, you will find in 365 MEATLESS MAIN DISH MEALS many wonderful ideas for planned informal get-togethers or impromptu suppers with people who just drop in. These of course are the nicest kind of dining experiences.

How often have you heard, "You don't mind if Harry and Martha stay for dinner, do you?"

Now if this question is posed by a well-brought-up, adorable youngster, it is always posed in front of the two would-be guests. In that case you have two more for dinner. Would you even entertain the idea of saying "No"?

So, to preserve your equilibrium and your budget under pressure, reach for 365 MEATLESS MAIN DISH MEALS. It's great 365 days a year.

SOUPS
AND
STEWS

———◆———

WEST COAST HALIBUT CHOWDER

3 tablespoons olive oil
1 clove garlic, minced
½ cup chopped onion
¾ cup minced green pepper
1 can (1 pound) tomatoes
1 can (8 ounces) tomato sauce
½ cup sliced ripe olives
1 bay leaf, crumbled
Pinch oregano
1 teaspoon salt
1 cup water
1 pound halibut steak, cut in 1-inch pieces

Heat oil in heavy saucepan. Add garlic, onion, and green pepper and cook until onion is tender. Add tomatoes, tomato sauce, olives, bay leaf, oregano, and salt. Cover and cook over low heat 50 minutes. Add water and cook 10 minutes longer. Add fish. Cook 5 to 10 minutes or until fish flakes easily with fork. If desired, serve with hot garlic bread.

YIELD: *4 servings.*

SEASIDE STEW

1 can (4 ounces) sliced mushrooms
1 tablespoon butter or margarine
1 can (10½ ounces) condensed cream of shrimp soup
1 soup can milk
2 cups cooked seafood (crab, whitefish, lobster, scallops, shrimp)
¼ cup shredded sharp cheese
2 tablespoons dry white wine, optional

Sauté drained mushrooms in butter in deep saucepan. Blend together mushroom liquid, soup, and milk; add to mushrooms. Heat to serving temperature. Blend in seafood and cheese. Heat until cheese is melted. Add wine just before serving.

YIELD: 4 servings.

VEGETABLE SALMON SOUP

> ½ cup coarsely chopped cucumber
> 2 tablespoons chopped onion
> 1 tablespoon butter or margarine
> ¼ teaspoon dried dillweed
> 1 can (10¾ ounces) condensed vegetable soup
> 1 soup can water
> ⅓ cup sour cream
> 1 can (8 ounces) salmon, drained and flaked

Cook cucumber and onion in butter until partially tender. Blend in remaining ingredients. Heat, stirring occasionally, but do not boil.

YIELD: 4 servings.

LOBSTER CHOWDER

> ¼ cup chopped onion
> 2 tablespoons butter or margarine
> 2 cans (11 ounces each) condensed Cheddar cheese
>   soup
> 1 soup can milk
> 1 soup can water
> 1 cup flaked cooked lobster
> 2 tablespoons chopped parsley
> ⅛ teaspoon pepper
> Paprika, optional

Cook onion in butter in deep saucepan until tender. Stir in soup until mixture is smooth; gradually blend in milk and water. Add lobster, parsley, and pepper. Heat; stir occasionally. If desired, sprinkle with paprika.

YIELD: *4 to 6 servings.*

LOBSTER MUSHROOM SOUP

> ¼ cup chopped onion
> 2 tablespoons butter or margarine
> 2 cans (10¾ ounces each) condensed cream of
>   mushroom soup
> 1 soup can milk
> 1 soup can water
> 1 can (6½ ounces) lobster or 1 cup flaked cooked lobster
> 2 tablespoons chopped parsley
> Dash pepper

Cook onion in butter until tender. Blend in soup and remaining ingredients. Heat; stir occasionally.

YIELD: *6 to 8 servings.*

QUICK MOCK BOUILLABAISSE

> 1 small onion, sliced
> 1 small clove garlic, minced
> ½ small bay leaf
> ¼ teaspoon dried leaf thyme
> 2 tablespoons olive oil
> 1 can (10¾ ounces) condensed tomato soup
> 1 soup can water
> 2 cups cooked seafood (crab, whitefish, lobster, shrimp)
> 1 teaspoon lemon juice
> Dash Tabasco
> 4 slices French bread, toasted

Cook onion, garlic, bay leaf, and thyme in olive oil in deep saucepan until onion is tender. Add soup, water, seafood, lemon juice, and Tabasco. Bring to boil. Cover; simmer 5 minutes. To serve; ladle soup over toast in bowls.

YIELD: *4 servings.*

MAINE FISH SOUP

½ cup chopped onion
1 tablespoon butter or margarine
1 can (10¾ ounces) condensed cream of chicken soup
1 can (10¾ ounces) condensed New England clam chowder
1½ soup cans water
1 cup flaked cooked whitefish or tuna (7-ounce can, drained and flaked) or shrimp (6-ounce can, drained)
1 tablespoon chopped parsley

Cook onion in butter until tender. Blend in remaining ingredients. Simmer a few minutes; stir often.

YIELD: *6 servings.*

MARDI GRAS GUMBO

1 can (10¾ ounces) condensed chicken gumbo soup
1 can (10¾ ounces) condensed tomato soup
1½ soup cans water
1 can (7¾ ounces) crab meat, flaked, drained
2 tablespoons sherry, optional
2 cups cooked rice

Combine ingredients except rice in deep saucepan. Heat to serving temperature, stirring occasionally. To serve, spoon rice into a tureen or individual soup bowls and pour in the soup.

YIELD: *6 to 8 servings.*

SEAFOOD AND TOMATO BOWL

¼ cup chopped onion
1 small clove garlic, minced
1 tablespoon butter or margarine
1 can (10¾ ounces) condensed Manhattan clam
  chowder
1 can (11 ounces) condensed tomato rice soup
1½ soup cans water
1 can (6½ or 7 ounces) tuna, drained and flaked
2 tablespoons chopped parsley

Cook onion and garlic in butter until onion is tender. Add remaining ingredients. Heat; stir often.

YIELD: *4 to 6 servings.*

SCALLOP STEW

3 cups milk
1 cup light cream
2 tablespoons butter or margarine
2 teaspoons sugar
½ teaspoon Worcestershire sauce
Salt
Pepper
1 pound scallops
Paprika
Parsley

Scald milk, cream, butter, sugar, and Worcestershire sauce in top of double boiler. Season with salt and pepper to taste. Mince scallops and add to scalded mixture. Cook 5 minutes only. Serve with dash of paprika and finely chopped parsley.

YIELD: *4 to 6 servings.*

EGGS

PIMIENTO EGG CURRY

3 tablespoons butter or margarine
1 small onion, minced
3 tablespoons flour
2 teaspoons curry powder
1 teaspoon salt
⅛ teaspoon pepper
2 cups milk
½ cup chicken broth or tomato juice
1 teaspoon grated lemon rind
1 can or jar (7 ounces) pimientos, diced
8 hard-cooked eggs, halved

Melt butter in saucepan; add onion and cook until tender. Blend in flour, curry powder, salt, and pepper. Gradually add milk and broth and cook, stirring constantly, until mixture thickens and comes to a boil. Remove from heat; add lemon rind, pimientos, and eggs. Continue to cook over low heat until mixture is warmed. Serve on Green Rice (below).

YIELD: *6 servings.*

GREEN RICE

3 cups hot cooked rice
2 tablespoons minced parsley
2 tablespoons chopped chives

Combine all ingredients.

YIELD: *6 servings.*

EGGS AROUND THE CLOCK

2 tablespoons butter or margarine
2 tablespoons flour
1½ cups milk
1 cup shredded Cheddar cheese
1 tablespoon grated Parmesan cheese
¼ teaspoon curry powder
¼ teaspoon celery salt
¼ teaspoon paprika
2 tablespoons sherry
2 cans (4½ ounces each) shrimp, drained

Melt butter in saucepan; blend in flour. Gradually add milk
and cook, stirring constantly, until mixture thickens and comes
to a boil. Blend in Cheddar and Parmesan cheese, curry powder, celery salt, and paprika; heat until cheese melts. Add
sherry and shrimp. Keep warm while preparing Scrambled
Eggs (below).

SCRAMBLED EGGS

8 eggs
¼ cup milk
1 tablespoon finely chopped parsley
1 teaspoon finely chopped onion

Combine eggs, milk, parsley, and onion; beat well. Pour into
hot, greased skillet. Cook, stirring, until eggs are set, lifting
from the bottom and sides as the mixture thickens. Transfer to
warm serving dish and top with sauce.

YIELD: *4 to 6 servings.*

CRAB-EGG FOO YONG

8 eggs
1 can (1 pound) bean sprouts, drained
1 can (7¾ ounces) crab meat
½ teaspoon salt
⅛ teaspoon pepper
½ cup chopped onion
6 tablespoons salad oil

Beat eggs until light. Stir in drained bean sprouts, crab meat, salt, pepper, and onion. Heat 1 tablespoon oil in a small skillet and pour in ½ cup of mixture. Cook until bottom is brown. Turn and brown other side. Keep warm and repeat, using 1 tablespoon oil for each cake.

YIELD: *6 servings.*

WESTERN SCRAMBLE

¼ cup chopped green pepper
¼ cup chopped onion
2 tablespoons butter or margarine
1 can (11 ounces) condensed Cheddar cheese soup
8 eggs, slightly beaten

Cook green pepper and onion in butter in a large skillet until vegetables are tender. Stir soup until smooth; blend in eggs. Add to vegetable mixture. Cook over low heat until eggs are set, stirring occasionally.

YIELD: *6 servings.*

DEVILED EGGS SPANISH STYLE

⅓ cup butter or margarine
⅓ cup chopped onion
⅓ cup chopped celery
3 tablespoons flour
1 teaspoon sugar
1 teaspoon salt
¼ teaspoon ground pepper
¼ teaspoon garlic salt
1 can (1 pound, 13 ounces) tomatoes
12 deviled egg halves
½ cup buttered bread crumbs

Melt butter in saucepan. Add onion and celery and cook until
onion is tender. Blend in flour and seasonings. Add tomatoes.
Cook until thickened, stirring constantly. Pour into shallow
1½-quart baking dish. Arrange deviled eggs in sauce. Top
with crumbs. Bake in 425° F. oven 15 minutes. Serve over toast,
rice, spaghetti, or noodles.

YIELD: 6 servings.

SHRIMP-EGG FOO YONG

3 tablespoons butter or margarine, divided
1 clove garlic
½ cup chopped onion
1 cup uncooked shrimp, shelled, deveined
6 eggs, slightly beaten
½ teaspoon salt
¼ teaspoon pepper

Melt 1 tablespoon butter in skillet; rub garlic clove around
skillet and remove. Add onion and shrimp and cook 5 minutes,

stirring occasionally. Remove from heat. Combine eggs, salt, and pepper; stir in shrimp mixture. Melt remaining 2 tablespoons butter in skillet. Pour in egg mixture. Cover; cook over low heat until eggs are set. Fold omelet in half; transfer to warm serving platter. Serve with Chinese Brown Sauce (below).

CHINESE BROWN SAUCE

3 tablespoons butter or margarine
1½ tablespoons cornstarch
1 teaspoon sugar
½ teaspoon salt
1 cup water
2 tablespoons soy sauce
1 cup drained bean sprouts

Melt butter in saucepan; blend in cornstarch, sugar, and salt. Stir in water and soy sauce and cook over low heat, stirring constantly, until thick and clear. Add bean sprouts and heat to serving temperature.

YIELD: *4 to 6 servings.*

ASPARAGUS AND MUSHROOMS WTH POACHED EGGS

1 package (10 ounces) frozen asparagus spears
1 can (3 or 4 ounces) sliced mushrooms
1 package (1 ounce) white sauce mix, prepared
4 English muffins, split
Butter
4 poached eggs
½ cup mayonnaise or salad dressing
2 tablespoons sour cream
2 tablespoons lemon juice

Cook asparagus according to package directions; drain well. Drain mushrooms; add to white sauce and heat in saucepan over low heat. Toast muffins and butter each half lightly; arrange on serving plate. Divide the asparagus spears among 4 muffin halves; cover with mushroom-white sauce. Place poached eggs on remaining 4 muffins. Combine remaining ingredients and spoon over poached eggs. Serve immediately.

YIELD: *4 servings.*

CLASSY CROQUETTES

⅓ cup butter or margarine
½ cup flour
1 teaspoon salt
⅛ teaspoon pepper
1 tall can (1⅔ cups) evaporated milk
4 egg yolks, slightly beaten
8 hard-cooked eggs, finely chopped
½ teaspoon almond extract
1 cup chopped blanched almonds, divided
2 egg whites, slightly beaten
2 tablespoons water
Oil for deep-fat frying

Melt butter or margarine in saucepan over low heat; blend in flour, salt, and pepper. Add milk and cook, stirring constantly, until mixture thickens and comes to a boil. Add a small amount of the hot mixture to the egg yolks, stirring constantly. Return to saucepan and cook 1 minute longer. Remove from heat; add hard-cooked eggs and almond extract. Line and oil a 9-inch-square pan; sprinkle with ½ cup chopped almonds. Spread egg mixture evenly in pan. Sprinkle with remaining almonds. Freeze for 2 hours until firm. Remove from pan and cut into 12 pieces. Combine egg whites and water. Dip pieces into egg-white mixture to coat well. Fry in deep fat (400° F.) until golden brown and heated through. Serve at once.

YIELD: *6 servings.*

EGGS TAMALE

¼ *cup butter or margarine*
½ *cup chopped onion*
¼ *cup chopped green pepper*
¼ *cup flour*
½ *teaspoon salt*
1 *can (1 pound) whole tomatoes*
1 *cup shredded American cheese*
2 *cups cooked noodles*
8 *hard-cooked eggs, sliced*

Melt butter in skillet. Add onion and green pepper; cook until tender. Blend in flour and salt. Add tomatoes and cook, stirring constantly, until thickened. Add cheese and stir until melted. Place half the cooked noodles in a 2-quart casserole; arrange half of the eggs over the noodles. Pour half of the tomato mixture over the eggs. Top with remaining noodles, sliced eggs; pour remaining tomato mixture over all. Bake in 350° F. oven 25 minutes or until thoroughly heated.

YIELD: *4 to 6 servings.*

QUICK EGG CURRY

1 *can (10¾ ounces) cream of mushroom soup*
⅓ *cup milk*
1 *teaspoon curry powder*
4 *hard-cooked eggs, sliced*
4 *slices toast*
Shredded coconut, toasted slivered almonds, chutney, or raisins

Combine soup and milk in saucepan; stir in curry powder. Heat. Add eggs, heat to serving temperature. Serve over toast with coconut, almonds, chutney, or raisins.

YIELD: *4 servings.*

CURRIED EGGS AND SHRIMP

6 hard-cooked eggs
¼ cup mayonnaise
¼ teaspoon curry powder
1 can (10½ ounces) condensed cream of shrimp soup
½ soup can milk
4 slices toast or toasted English muffin halves

Cut eggs in half lengthwise. Scoop out and mash yolk; stir in mayonnaise and curry powder. Refill egg halves. Combine soup and milk in saucepan. Heat to serving temperature. Place 3 egg halves on each piece of toast or English muffin. Spoon soup over top.

YIELD: *4 servings.*

EGG CROQUETTES

1 can (10¾ ounces) condensed cream of chicken or
    mushroom soup, divided
8 hard-cooked eggs, sieved or very finely chopped
¼ cup fine dry bread crumbs
2 tablespoons minced parsley
2 tablespoons minced onion
½ teaspoon salt
Dash pepper
2 tablespoons shortening
⅓ cup milk

Mix ¼ cup undiluted soup with eggs, bread crumbs, parsley, onion, and seasonings; form into 6 croquettes. (If mixture is difficult to handle, chill before shaping.) Roll in additional bread crumbs. Fry croquettes slowly in shortening until browned. Meanwhile, combine remaining soup with milk in saucepan. Heat to serving temperature, stirring occasionally. Serve as sauce over croquettes.

YIELD: *3 servings.*

EGG FOO YONG

2 tablespoons butter or margarine
1 can (1 pound) bean sprouts, drained (reserve liquid
for sauce)
½ cup chopped onion
½ cup finely chopped celery
1 tablespoon finely chopped green pepper
1 teaspoon salt
1 teaspoon soy sauce
4 eggs, slightly beaten
Salad oil for frying

Melt butter in saucepan. Add bean sprouts, onion, celery, and green pepper. Cover and cook about 5 minutes until onion is tender. Cool slightly. Add salt and soy sauce to eggs; beat with fork until well blended. Combine cooled vegetables and egg mixture. Spoon about one fourth of mixture into hot oil, spreading to form a cake 5 inches in diameter. Cook until brown, about 4 minutes on each side, carefully turning once. Drain and serve with Bean Sauce (below).

YIELD: *2 servings.*

BEAN SAUCE

1 tablespoon cornstarch
1 teaspoon sugar
¾ cup liquid from canned bean sprouts
¼ cup soy sauce

Combine cornstarch, sugar, and bean sprout liquid in a saucepan. Cook, stirring constantly, until clear and thickened. Add soy sauce; heat.

ORIENTAL DELIGHT (SHRIMP OMELET)

2 tablespoons butter or margarine
1½ cups finely chopped onion
2 cups diced cooked shrimp
¾ cup drained bean sprouts
6 eggs, beaten
1 quart cooking oil
1 cup beef bouillon
1 tablespoon cornstarch
2 teaspoons soy sauce

Melt butter in skillet; add onion and cook until tender. Add shrimp and bean sprouts. Add shrimp mixture to beaten eggs in a large bowl. Heat the cooking oil to 375° F. in a deep-fat fryer or electric frypan. Drop the shrimp-egg mixture into the hot oil, using about ¼ cup at a time. Cook until omelets are golden brown on one side, turn and brown the other side; about 5 minutes. Remove omelets from hot oil and drain on absorbent paper; place on hot platter to serve. Combine beef bouillon, cornstarch, and soy sauce in a saucepan. Cook over low heat until clear and thickened, stirring constantly. Serve over the omelets.

YIELD: *6 servings.*

CHEESE AND ANCHOVY OMELET

4 eggs, separated
½ teaspoon salt
Dash pepper
½ cup milk
⅓ cup wheat germ
1 tablespoon butter or margarine

Beat egg yolks until thick; add seasonings, milk, and wheat germ. Beat egg whites until stiff; fold in egg yolk mixture. Melt butter in a 9-inch ovenproof skillet; pour in omelet mixture. Cook over low heat 3 to 5 minutes until omelet puffs up, and bottom is brown. Place in 350° F. oven; bake 5 minutes. Remove and pour Cheese and Anchovy Sauce (below) over one half of omelet, then fold over. Return to oven and bake 5 minutes longer.

YIELD: *2 servings.*

CHEESE AND ANCHOVY SAUCE

4 tablespoons butter or margarine
4 tablespoons flour
¼ teaspoon salt
2 cups milk
½ pound shredded American cheese
2 tablespoons chopped anchovy fillets

Melt butter in saucepan; blend in flour and salt. Gradually add milk and cook, stirring constantly, until mixture thickens and comes to a boil. Add cheese; stir until melted. Stir in anchovies.

NOODLE OMELET

4 ounces medium noodles
2 tablespoons chopped onion
3 tablespoons butter or margarine
3 eggs
2 tablespoons water
½ teaspoon salt
⅛ teaspoon pepper

Cook noodles in boiling salted water according to package directions. Drain well. Cook onion in butter in saucepan until tender. Stir in noodles. Beat together eggs, water, salt, and pepper; pour over noodles in skillet. Cook rapidly, lifting mixture with fork, at the same time tipping skillet to let uncooked mixture flow to bottom of skillet. Cook until the bottom is browned. Fold in half.

YIELD: *3 servings.*

APPLE SPICE OMELET

2 apples, peeled, cored and thinly sliced
2 tablespoons butter or margarine
2 tablespoons brown sugar
½ teaspoon cinnamon
Dash nutmeg
2 eggs
2 tablespoons water
¼ teaspoon salt
1 teaspoon butter

Cook apples in 2 tablespoons butter in small skillet until tender, about 5 minutes. Sprinkle brown sugar, cinnamon, and nutmeg over apples and mix well. Beat together eggs, water, and salt. Heat 1 teaspoon butter in small skillet. Pour in egg mixture. With a spatula or fork, carefully draw cooked portions at edges toward center, so that uncooked portions flow to bottom. Cook until the bottom is browned. Place ¼ cup apples in center of omelet, fold on plate. Place ¼ cup apples and juice on top of omelet and serve.

YIELD: *1 serving.*

GOLDEN RAISIN OMELET

¼ cup brown sugar
1 teaspoon grated orange rind
1 teaspoon dry mustard
2 tablespoons cornstarch
1½ cups orange juice
¾ cup seedless raisins
1 orange, sectioned
2 eggs
2 tablespoons water
¼ teaspoon salt
1 teaspoon butter

Blend brown sugar, orange rind, mustard, and cornstarch together in a small saucepan. Stir in orange juice. Bring to a boil, and cook, stirring constantly until mixture is clear and thickened, about 5 minutes. Add raisins and orange sections, cook 4 to 5 minutes longer. Beat together eggs, water, and salt with a fork. Heat butter in small skillet. Pour in egg mixture. With a spatula or fork, carefully draw cooked portions at edges toward center, so that uncooked portions flow to the bottom. Cook until the bottom is browned. Serve omelet folded on plate with sauce spooned over top.

YIELD: *1 serving.*

SEAFOOD OMELET

1 can (8 ounces) peas
1 can (8 ounces) salmon
1 can (10¾ ounces) condensed cream of mushroom
 soup
9 eggs
½ cup water
1 teaspoon salt
3 tablespoons butter or margarine

Combine peas with liquid, salmon, and undiluted soup in a saucepan. Heat to serving temperature; keep warm. Beat eggs, water, and salt together until light and foamy. Heat butter in a large skillet. Use ¼ cup of the egg mixture for each omelet. When omelets are set and lightly browned on the bottom, place 2 tablespoons of filling in the center of each; fold.

YIELD: 6 servings.

FISH FLAKE OMELET

2 tablespoons lemon juice
2 cups flaked cooked fish (flounder, halibut, cod)
4 eggs, separated
½ cup milk
2 tablespoons minced onion
1 tablespoon minced parsley
¾ teaspoon salt
⅛ teaspoon pepper
2 tablespoons butter or margarine

Add lemon juice to fish. Beat egg yolks thoroughly; stir in milk, onion, parsley, salt, and pepper. Beat egg whites until stiff, but not dry. Fold into cooked fish. Melt butter in a large skillet; pour in egg mixture. Cook over low heat until delicate brown on bottom (about 10 minutes). Place in 300° F. oven about 10 minutes, or until top is firm and dry to the touch. Cut part way through omelet at center, fold in half and slip onto heated platter.

YIELD: *6 servings.*

PRINCESS OMELET

> *1 package (10 ounces) frozen asparagus*
> *4 eggs*
> *¼ cup sour cream*
> *2 teaspoons minced onion*
> *⅛ teaspoon crushed red pepper*
> *½ teaspoon salt*
> *1 package (3 ounces) cream cheese, cut into ¼-inch*
> *   cubes*
> *1 tablespoon butter or margarine*

Cook asparagus spears according to package directions; drain and reserve, keeping warm. Combine eggs, sour cream, onion, red pepper, and salt; beat well. Add cream cheese. Melt butter in skillet; pour in egg mixture. As the mixture thickens at the edges draw these portions with a fork toward the center, so that the uncooked portions flow to the bottom. When eggs are set, arrange cooked asparagus on half of the omelet. Fold over and transfer to a warm serving dish. Serve at once.

YIELD: *2 servings.*

WESTERN RODEO OMELET

> *¼ cup chopped green pepper*
> *¼ cup chopped scallions*
> *¼ cup butter or margarine*
> *1 can (10½ ounces) condensed cream of celery soup*
> *8 eggs, slightly beaten*

Cook green pepper and scallions in butter in large skillet until tender. Blend soup and eggs; add to skillet. Cook over low heat until eggs are set, stirring occasionally.

YIELD: *6 servings.*

SUNSHINE OMELET

1 can (10¾ ounces) condensed cream of mushroom
     soup
2 cups cooked diced potatoes
1 package (10 ounces) frozen mixed vegetables, cooked
½ cup diced American cheese
Salt
Pepper
9 eggs
½ cup water
1 teaspoon salt
3 tablespoons butter or margarine

Combine undiluted soup, potatoes, vegetables, cheese, salt, and pepper in a saucepan. Cook over low heat until cheese is melted. Keep warm. Beat together eggs, water, and salt until light and foamy. Heat butter in a large skillet. Use ¼ cup of the egg mixture for each omelet. When omelets are set and lightly browned on the bottom, place 2 tablespoons of filling in the center of each; fold.

YIELD: *6 servings.*

MUSHROOM-CHEESE OMELET

¼ pound processed American cheese, shredded
¼ cup milk
⅛ teaspoon pepper

4 eggs, separated
¼ teaspoon salt
3 tablespoons butter or margarine, divided
¼ pound mushrooms, sliced

Heat cheese and milk in saucepan over low heat until cheese is melted, stirring constantly. Add pepper to egg yolks and beat until thick and lemon-colored. Gradually pour cheese sauce into yolks, stirring constantly. Add salt to whites and beat until stiff but not dry. Fold yolk mixture into whites, gently but thoroughly. Heat 1 tablespoon butter in a 9- or 10-inch ovenproof skillet. Cook over low heat 3 to 5 minutes until omelet puffs up and bottom is brown. Place in a 350° F. oven; bake 10 minutes. While omelet is baking, cook mushrooms in remaining 2 tablespoons butter about 5 minutes and spoon over the omelet. Fold and serve immediately.

YIELD: *3 servings.*

ROSY RINGED OMELET

1 package (4¾ ounces) strawberry-flavored Danish
  Dessert Mix
1 can (1 pound) pineapple slices
4 eggs
2 tablespoons water
¼ teaspoon salt
1 teaspoon butter

Prepare Danish Dessert according to package directions for pudding, using pineapple syrup for part of liquid. Chill thoroughly. Mix eggs, water, and salt with fork. Heat butter in a small skillet. Pour in egg mixture. With spatula or fork, carefully draw cooked portions at edges toward center, so that uncooked portions flow to bottom. Cook until omelet is browned on bottom. Remove pan from heat and spread half of omelet with 2 tablespoons Danish Dessert. Place pineapple slice over

Danish Dessert. Fold omelet and slip out onto serving plate. Spread 2 tablespoons more of Danish Dessert on top of omelet and place pineapple slice on top. Serve immediately.

YIELD: *4 servings.*

CHINESE OMELETS WITH HOT SOY SAUCE

1 can (14½ ounces) mixed chop suey vegetables
1 can (3 or 4 ounces) sliced mushrooms
⅓ cup chopped onion
⅓ cup finely sliced celery
2 tablespoons chopped parsley
⅔ cup instant nonfat dry milk
⅓ cup water
6 eggs
½ teaspoon salt
¼ teaspoon pepper
¼ teaspoon garlic salt
1 tablespoon soy sauce
¼ cup butter or margarine

Drain vegetables and mushrooms; reserve 1½ cups liquid for Hot Soy Sauce. Add drained vegetables to onion, celery, and parsley. Beat nonfat dry milk, water, and eggs; add seasonings, then the vegetables. Melt butter in a large skillet; when hot add ¼ cup mixture for each omelet. Turn when browned on bottom. Remove and keep in warm oven until ready to serve. Serve with Hot Soy Sauce (below).

YIELD: *8 servings.*

HOT SOY SAUCE

1½ tablespoons cornstarch
1 tablespoon sugar

> *2 tablespoons soy sauce*
> *1½ cups reserved vegetable and mushroom liquid*

Mix cornstarch and sugar in a small saucepan; blend in soy sauce and vegetable liquid. Cook, stirring constantly, until thickened and clear. Serve hot with the omelets.

SALMON NEWBURG

> *4 egg yolks, slightly beaten*
> *1 cup heavy cream*
> *½ teaspoon salt*
> *1 can (1 pound) salmon, drained and flaked*
> *2 tablespoons sherry*

Combine egg yolks, cream, and salt in top of double boiler. Cook over simmering water until thickened, stirring constantly. Add salmon and sherry; heat thoroughly. Serve at once in pastry shells or over hot crisp waffles.

YIELD: *4 servings.*

EGGS ORIENTAL

> *5 hard-cooked eggs*
> *1 can (10¾ ounces) condensed cream of mushroom*
>   *soup*
> *2 tablespoons chopped pimiento*
> *⅔ cup evaporated milk*
> *½ teaspoon curry powder*
> *Bite-sized shredded rice cereal*

Chop 4 of the hard-cooked eggs and slice remaining egg for garnish. Blend soup with pimiento, evaporated milk, and curry powder in a saucepan. Stir over low heat until hot. Add chopped eggs and heat to serving temperature. Meanwhile heat rice cereal in 300° F. oven to crisp. Serve curried eggs over cereal; garnish with slices of hard-cooked egg.

YIELD: *4 servings.*

EGGS RANCHO ON PEPPER CORN BREAD

1 tablespoon butter
1 tablespoon minced onion
¾ teaspoon chili powder
1 tablespoon flour
1 can (10¾ ounces) condensed tomato soup
½ cup evaporated milk
6 hard-cooked eggs, quartered

Melt butter in a saucepan. Add onion and chili powder and cook until onion is tender. Remove from heat and blend in flour. Stir in tomato soup, then evaporated milk. Heat, stirring occasionally. Add eggs and heat to serving temperature, stirring gently. Serve over squares of hot Pepper Corn Bread (below).

YIELD: *6 servings.*

PEPPER CORN BREAD

1 package (10 ounces) corn bread mix
¼ cup finely chopped green pepper

Prepare corn bread mix according to package directions. Stir in green pepper. Bake according to package directions. When ready to serve, cut corn bread into 6 pieces and top with Eggs Rancho.

ITALIAN EGG PIE

Pastry for 1 (9-inch) pie shell
6 eggs
¼ cup milk
1 can (6½ or 7 ounces) tuna, drained and flaked
½ pound mozzarella cheese, grated
¼ teaspoon salt
¼ teaspoon pepper
½ teaspoon dried leaf basil
½ teaspoon dried leaf oregano

Line a 9-inch pie pan with pastry; trim edge and flute. Beat eggs and milk until blended. Stir in remaining ingredients. Turn into unbaked crust. Bake in a 425° F. oven, 35 to 40 minutes. To serve, cut into wedges.

YIELD: *6 servings.*

EGGS FLORENTINE

2 packages (10 ounces each) frozen chopped spinach
6 eggs
1 can (10¾ ounces) condensed cream of mushroom
     soup
½ cup milk
1 cup shredded American cheese

Cook spinach according to package directions. Drain well and place in a 10×6×2-inch baking dish. Make 6 indentations in spinach. Break an egg into each hollow. Combine soup and milk and pour around eggs completely covering spinach; sprinkle with cheese. Bake in a 350° F. oven 25 to 30 minutes or until eggs are done.

YIELD: *6 servings.*

SHERRIED EGGS À LA OZARKS

DEVILED EGGS:

>9 *hard-cooked eggs*
>⅓ *cup mayonnaise or salad dressing*
>2 *tablespoons sweet pickle relish*
>2 *tablespoons grated Parmesan cheese*
>2 *teaspoons salad mustard*
>¼ *teaspoon salt*
>2 *cans (4½ ounces) shrimp, drained*
>2 *cans (3 or 4 ounces) sliced mushrooms, drained*
>1 *can (4 ounces) water chestnuts, drained and thinly*
>   *sliced*

SAUCE:

>1 *can (10¾ ounces) condensed cream of chicken soup*
>1 *cup sour cream*
>½ *cup dry sherry*
>1 *tablespoon minced parsley*
>2 *teaspoons granulated chicken bouillon*
>1 *teaspoon minced onion*
>3 *tablespoons chopped pimiento*
>1 *tablespoon soy sauce*
>½ *cup pecan halves*

Cut eggs in half lengthwise; remove yolks. Mash yolks and combine with mayonnaise, pickle relish, cheese, mustard, and salt. Fill egg whites with yolk mixture. Place shrimp in a 7×11-inch baking dish; top with a layer of mushrooms and a layer of water chestnuts. Place deviled eggs on top. Combine remaining ingredients except pecans in bowl; mix well. Pour into baking dish; sprinkle with pecans. Bake in a 350° F. oven 25 minutes.

YIELD: *6 servings.*

EASY EGG BAKE

1 can (10¾ ounces) condensed cream of chicken or
  mushroom soup
⅓ cup milk
6 thin slices tomato
6 slices buttered toast or toasted English muffin halves
6 eggs, poached
1 tablespoon minced parsley

Blend soup and milk in saucepan. Heat to serving temperature, stirring occasionally. Meanwhile, place a slice of tomato on each slice of toast or muffin half; top with poached egg. Pour sauce over eggs. Sprinkle with minced parsley.

YIELD: *6 servings.*

GOLDEN EGG SALAD CASSEROLE

6 hard-cooked eggs, chopped
2 tablespoons diced pimiento
½ cup diced celery
1½ cups crushed soda crackers, divided
1 cup mayonnaise or salad dressing
¼ cup milk
¼ to ½ teaspoon salt
½ teaspoon garlic salt
¼ teaspoon pepper
2 tablespoons melted butter or margarine

Combine eggs, pimiento, celery, 1 cup of the cracker crumbs, mayonnaise, milk, and seasonings. Spread in greased 1-quart shallow casserole or 9-inch pie pan. Top with remaining ½ cup cracker crumbs blended with the butter or margarine. Bake in a 400° F. oven until golden brown, about 25 minutes. Serve hot.

YIELD: 6 servings.

CURRIED EGGS ON FRIED RICE WAIKIKI

1 can (9 ounces) crushed pineapple
¼ cup butter or margarine
¼ cup sliced scallions
¼ cup flour
1 tablespoon curry powder
½ teaspoon salt
1 tall can (1⅔ cups) evaporated milk
2 tablespoons 1-inch-long strips pimiento
6 hard-cooked eggs, sliced

Drain pineapple; reserve liquid. Set pineapple aside to use in Fried Rice Waikiki (below). Melt butter in a saucepan. Add scallions and cook over low heat 5 minutes. Remove from heat and blend in flour, curry powder, and salt. Gradually stir in evaporated milk. Add enough water to reserved pineapple liquid to make ½ cup, then blend into milk mixture. Stir in pimiento. Cook, stirring occasionally, over low heat until sauce is thickened, about 15 minutes. Gently stir in sliced eggs and heat, without stirring, 3 to 4 minutes longer. Serve over Fried Rice Waikiki (below).

FRIED RICE WAIKIKI

¼ cup butter
2 cups packaged precooked rice

> 1½ *cups water*
> ½ *teaspoon salt*

Melt butter in a frypan that has a tight-fitting cover. Stir in rice and cook over medium heat until rice is golden brown, stirring occasionally. Add water and salt, stirring well. Bring to a boil, then cover and reduce heat to simmer for 5 minutes. Just before serving toss lightly with the drained crushed pineapple.

YIELD: *4 servings.*

EGGS 'N' CHIPS CASSEROLE

> *8 hard-cooked eggs, coarsely chopped*
> 1½ *cups chopped celery*
> ¼ *cup coarsely chopped walnuts*
> *2 tablespoons minced green pepper*
> *1 teaspoon minced onion*
> ½ *teaspoon salt*
> ¼ *teaspoon pepper*
> ⅔ *cup mayonnaise or salad dressing*
> *1 cup shredded Cheddar cheese*
> *1 cup crushed potato chips*

Combine eggs, celery, walnuts, green pepper, onion, salt, pepper, and mayonnaise or salad dressing. Toss lightly. Turn into a greased 1½-quart baking dish. Sprinkle with cheese and top with potato chips. Bake in a 375° F. oven 25 minutes or until thoroughly heated.

YIELD: *6 servings.*

BLUSHING EGGS À LA TOREADOR

> 8 hard-cooked eggs
> ¼ cup shredded sharp Cheddar cheese
> 1 can (3½ ounces) French fried onion rings
> 1 can (1 pound) red kidney beans, drained
> 1 can (10½ ounces) tomato purée
> ½ cup mayonnaise or salad dressing
> 1 teaspoon chili powder
> ½ teaspoon salt
> ⅛ teaspoon pepper

Cut eggs in half lengthwise; place in a 2-quart shallow baking dish. Sprinkle with cheese; top with half of the onion rings. Pour the kidney beans over eggs. Combine the tomato purée, mayonnaise, and seasonings. Pour over the ingredients in the dish; top with remaining onion rings. Bake in a 350° F. oven 35 to 40 minutes or until thoroughly heated.

YIELD: 4 to 6 servings.

BAKED EGGS SAVORY

> ¼ cup salad oil
> ¼ pound mushrooms, sliced
> ¼ cup flour
> 1¼ teaspoons salt
> ⅛ teaspoon paprika
> 2 cups milk
> ⅓ cup pimiento cheese spread
> 2 tablespoons chopped green pepper
> 6 hard-cooked eggs, sliced
> 1 cup small bread cubes
> 2 tablespoons butter or margarine, melted
> 1 teaspoon minced onion

Heat oil in saucepan; add mushrooms and cook 5 minutes. Blend in flour, salt, and paprika. Gradually add milk and cook, stirring constantly, until mixture thickens and comes to a boil. Stir in cheese and green pepper. Place eggs in shallow greased 1½-quart casserole; cover with sauce. Toss bread cubes in butter; stir in onion. Sprinkle over casserole. Place under broiler until golden brown, about 10 minutes.

YIELD: *6 servings.*

DE LUXE EGG CASSEROLE

¼ cup butter or margarine
½ pound mushrooms, sliced
¼ cup flour
1 teaspoon onion salt
1 teaspoon celery salt
¾ teaspoon salt
¼ teaspoon ground pepper
3 cups milk
1 package (1 pound) frozen French fries, unthawed
¼ pound shredded Cheddar cheese
8 hard-cooked eggs, chopped

Melt butter in skillet; add mushrooms and cook until tender, about 5 minutes. Blend in flour and seasonings. Gradually add milk and cook, stirring constantly, until mixture thickens and comes to a boil. Stir in frozen French fries and cheese. Pour half the mixture into a greased 2-quart baking dish. Top with eggs. Pour in remaining mixture. Bake in a 400° F. oven about 30 minutes.

YIELD: *6 servings.*

EGGS AND OYSTERS AU GRATIN

1 can (10¾ ounces) condensed oyster stew
¼ cup milk
1 cup shredded sharp Cheddar cheese
2 hard-cooked eggs, sliced
1 pound asparagus or broccoli, cooked and well drained
Dash paprika

Combine oyster stew and milk in a saucepan. Heat, stirring constantly. Add cheese; continue to cook until cheese is melted. Fold in eggs. Pour over hot asparagus or broccoli. Garnish with paprika.

YIELD: *4 servings.*

BAKED EGGS WITH RICE AND CHEESE SAUCE

4 tablespoons butter or margarine
½ cup finely chopped green pepper
½ cup sliced fresh mushrooms
3 tablespoons flour
1 teaspoon salt
⅛ teaspoon pepper
2 cups milk
1 cup shredded American cheese
3 cups cooked rice
8 eggs

Melt butter in saucepan; add green pepper and mushrooms and cook until tender. Blend in flour, salt, and pepper. Gradually add milk and cook, stirring constantly, until mixture thickens and comes to a boil. Remove from heat; add cheese and stir until melted. Combine 1½ cups of the sauce with the cooked rice. Spread the rice mixture evenly in a well-greased 13×9-inch shallow baking dish. Make 8 indentations with back of a spoon. Carefully break an egg into each indentation. Bake in a 350° F. oven 20 to 25 minutes or until eggs cook to desired doneness. Serve with remaining cheese and mushroom sauce.

YIELD: *8 servings.*

EGG-ASPARAGUS SPRING CASSEROLE

1 pound fresh asparagus or 1 package (10 ounces)
   frozen cut asparagus
4 hard-cooked eggs
1 teaspoon minced onion
1 can (10¾ ounces) condensed cream of mushroom
   soup
¾ cup milk
1 cup coarse soft bread crumbs
2 tablespoons melted butter
½ cup shredded American cheese
6 slices toast

Cook asparagus; slice eggs. Combine onion, soup, and milk. Beat to blend. Heat soup mixture until smooth. Combine bread crumbs, butter, and cheese. Cube toast into 1-inch pieces; arrange half of toast cubes across bottom of a 1½-quart baking dish. Arrange cooked asparagus over toast. Top with remaining toast cubes and sliced eggs. Pour soup mixture over all. Sprinkle with cheese-bread crumb topping. Bake at 350° F. for 15 minutes.

YIELD: *4 servings.*

EGGS LA MADELINE

3 tablespoons butter or margarine
3 tablespoons flour
1 teaspoon salt
¼ teaspoon white pepper
¼ teaspoon dried leaf marjoram
1½ cups light cream
1 package (10 ounces) frozen chopped spinach
4 poached eggs
¼ cup grated Parmesan cheese

Melt butter in saucepan; blend in flour, salt, pepper, and marjoram. Gradually add cream and cook, stirring constantly, until mixture thickens and comes to a boil. Set aside. Cook spinach
according to package directions; drain well. Spread in a greased
shallow baking dish. Top with poached eggs. Pour sauce over
all. Sprinkle with cheese. Place under broiler until lightly
browned, about 5 minutes.

YIELD: *4 servings.*

EGG PIE TYROLESE

Butter or margarine
3 medium tomatoes, sliced ½ inch thick
2 tablespoons anchovy butter
1½ teaspoons chopped parsley
1 tablespoon chopped chives
6 tablespoons bread crumbs
2 tablespoons melted butter or margarine
6 hard-cooked eggs, sliced
6 eggs

> *1 teaspoon salt*
> *¼ teaspoon pepper*
> *2 cups light cream*

Generously butter a 9×9-inch shallow baking dish. Cover bottom with tomato slices. Spread each slice lightly with anchovy butter. Sprinkle parsley and chives over tomatoes. Toss bread crumbs with melted butter. Cover tomatoes with alternate layers of egg slices and buttered bread crumbs. Beat eggs thoroughly with salt and pepper; add cream and mix well. Pour over the tomato-egg mixture. Bake in 375° F. oven 35 minutes or until the custard is set. Serve piping hot.

YIELD: *6 servings.*

EGGS GERMAINE

> *4 tablespoons butter or margarine, divided*
> *¼ cup flour*
> *1 teaspoon salt, divided*
> *¼ teaspoon pepper*
> *¼ teaspoon nutmeg*
> *2 cups milk*
> *8 hard-cooked eggs*
> *1 package (10 ounces) frozen chopped spinach, cooked*
> *and drained*
> *2 tablespoons grated Parmesan cheese*
> *2 tablespoons butter*

Melt butter in saucepan; blend in flour, ½ teaspoon salt, pepper, and nutmeg. Gradually add milk and cook, stirring constantly, until mixture thickens and comes to a boil. Remove from heat and reserve. Cut eggs in half lengthwise; remove yolks. Sieve yolks, combine with spinach and remaining ½ teaspoon salt. Refill whites with spinach mixture, placing filled eggs in a 1½-quart shallow baking dish. Pour reserved sauce over eggs. Sprinkle with Parmesan cheese and dot with remaining 2 tablespoons butter. Broil for 5 minutes or until lightly browned. If desired, serve over hot toast points.

YIELD: *5 to 6 servings.*

SPRINGTIME DEVILED EGG CASSEROLE

6 hard-cooked eggs
1 teaspoon salt, divided
¼ teaspoon Tabasco, divided
¼ cup mayonnaise
¼ teaspoon paprika
1 teaspoon prepared mustard
2 packages (10 ounces each) frozen asparagus
2 tablespoons butter or margarine
2 tablespoons flour
1¼ cups milk
1 cup shredded Cheddar cheese

Cut eggs in half lengthwise; remove yolks. Sieve yolks and combine with ½ teaspoon salt, ⅛ teaspoon Tabasco, mayonnaise, paprika, and mustard. Refill whites. Reserve. Cook asparagus according to package directions; drain and reserve. Melt butter in saucepan; blend in flour and remaining ½ teaspoon salt. Gradually add milk and cook, stirring constantly, until mixture thickens and comes to a boil. Add remaining ⅛ teaspoon Tabasco and cheese; stir until cheese melts. Place hot asparagus in shallow baking dish; top with deviled egg halves. Spoon hot sauce over all. Bake in 375° F. oven 10 minutes.

YIELD: *6 servings.*

DAISY EGG MOLD

12 hard-cooked eggs
2 envelopes unflavored gelatin
½ cup cold water
1 cup chicken broth
1½ cups mayonnaise or salad dressing
2 tablespoons lemon juice
1½ teaspoons salt, divided
⅛ teaspoon Tabasco
1¼ cups finely chopped parsley
½ cup finely chopped green pepper
2 tablespoons minced onion
1 teaspoon Ac'cent or monosodium glutamate
Salad greens

Cut 6 eggs lengthwise in slices, reserving center slices for garnish. Separate remaining eggs. Force yolks through sieve and set aside; finely chop the whites and reserve. Soften gelatin in cold water. Heat chicken broth to boiling and add gelatin, stirring until dissolved. Place ⅓ cup of the gelatin mixture in bottom of a 1½-quart ring mold. Arrange center egg slices in circle in bottom of mold. Chill until almost set. Combine sieved egg yolks, mayonnaise, lemon juice, ½ teaspoon salt, and Tabasco with half the remaining gelatin. Spoon mixture on top of egg slices. Sprinkle with the parsley and green pepper. Chill until partially set. Combine remaining gelatin, reserved chopped egg whites, onion, 1 teaspoon salt, and Ac'cent; spoon into mold. Chill until set; at least 6 hours. Unmold on salad greens on a large platter.

YIELD: *8 to 10 servings.*

TUNA SOUFFLÉ

¼ cup butter or margarine
¼ cup flour
½ teaspoon powdered mustard
¼ teaspoon salt
Dash cayenne
1 cup milk
6 eggs, separated
1 tablespoon chopped parsley
1 can (6½ or 7 ounces) tuna, drained and flaked

Melt butter in saucepan; blend in flour and seasonings. Add milk gradually and cook until thick and smooth, stirring constantly. Stir a little of hot sauce into egg yolks; add to remaining sauce, stirring constantly. Add parsley and tuna. Beat egg whites until stiff, but not dry. Fold into tuna mixture. Turn into a greased, 2-quart casserole. Bake in a 350° F. oven 45 minutes or until soufflé is firm in the center.

YIELD: 6 servings.

SHRIMP CURRY SOUFFLÉ

1 can (4½ ounces) shrimp, drained
2 tablespoons butter or margarine
¼ cup finely chopped onion
1 clove garlic, minced
2 tablespoons flour
¼ teaspoon powdered ginger
1 teaspoon curry powder
¾ cup light cream
¼ teaspoon salt
1 cup cottage cheese
3 eggs, separated
2 teaspoons chopped parsley

Chop shrimp coarsely. Melt butter in a saucepan; add onion and garlic and cook about 1 minute. Combine flour, ginger, and curry; blend into butter mixture. Add cream and cook, stirring constantly, until mixture thickens and comes to a boil. Remove from heat; stir in salt. Beat together cottage cheese and egg yolks. Stir vigorously into hot mixture; add shrimp and parsley. Beat egg whites until stiff; fold into shrimp mixture. Turn into a 1½-quart casserole. Bake in 300° F. oven 50 minutes to 1 hour or until knife inserted in the center comes out clean.

YIELD: *4 servings.*

SALMON SOUFFLÉ

1 can (8 ounces) salmon
Milk
1 cup liquid (liquid from canned salmon plus milk to
*   make volume)*
2 tablespoons butter
2 tablespoons flour
½ teaspoon salt
½ cup mayonnaise
3 eggs, separated

Drain salmon; add enough milk to salmon liquid to make 1 cup; reserve. Melt butter in saucepan; blend in flour and salt. Add combined milk and salmon liquid gradually, and cook, stirring constantly, until mixture thickens and comes to a boil. Remove from heat and stir in mayonnaise. Whip egg yolks until light in color and stir into slightly cooled sauce. Add salmon. Beat egg whites until stiff but not dry. Fold salmon mixture into egg whites. Turn into an ungreased 1½-quart casserole. Place casserole in a shallow pan of hot water and bake in a 350° F. oven 45 minutes or until soufflé is puffed and set. Serve immediately.

YIELD: *4 servings.*

CHEESE

ROSY RAREBIT

½ pound process cheese
½ cup evaporated milk
1 can (10¾ ounces) undiluted condensed tomato soup
2 teaspoons instant minced onion
⅛ teaspoon pepper
¼ teaspoon dried leaf oregano

Shred cheese or cut into cubes. Combine in top of double boiler with evaporated milk. Heat over hot water until cheese is melted, stirring occasionally. Mix together tomato soup, onion, pepper, and oregano. When cheese is melted, stir tomato soup mixture into melted cheese; heat. Serve on crisp toast or crackers or rusks.

YIELD: *6 servings.*

SALMON RAREBIT

2 tablespoons butter or margarine
2 tablespoons flour
1½ cups milk
⅓ cup shredded Cheddar cheese
2 tablespoons chopped ripe olives
1 can (8 ounces) salmon, drained and coarsely flaked
4 slices toast

Melt butter in saucepan; blend in flour. Gradually add milk and cook, stirring constantly, until mixture thickens and comes to a boil. Add cheese and olives; stir until cheese melts. Spread salmon on toast; top with cheese-olive sauce.

YIELD: *4 servings.*

EASY TOMATO CHEESE RAREBIT

1 can (10¾ ounces) condensed tomato soup
¼ teaspoon Tabasco
½ teaspoon dry mustard
½ teaspoon paprika
½ cup water
1 medium onion, sliced
2 cups shredded American cheese
1 egg, separated

Combine tomato soup, Tabasco, dry mustard, paprika, and water in top of double boiler. Add onion; cook until onion is tender, about 10 minutes. Add cheese to tomato mixture, place over boiling water, and stir until melted. Gradually stir small amount of hot mixture into beaten egg yolk. Beat egg white until stiff, but not dry. Add egg yolk-cheese mixture, stirring to blend well. Return to cheese mixture and cook 5 minutes longer. Serve on toast points or crackers.

YIELD: *4 to 6 servings.*

COTTAGE CHEESE DINNER CASSEROLE

8 ounces medium noodles
1½ cups creamed cottage cheese
2 cups sour cream
2 tablespoons chopped chives or scallions
1 teaspoon salt
⅛ teaspoon pepper
1 cup fresh bread crumbs
2 tablespoons butter
½ cup shredded Cheddar cheese

Cook noodles in boiling salted water according to package directions. Drain and combine with cottage cheese, sour cream, chives, salt, and pepper. Turn into a greased 1½-quart casserole. Brown bread crumbs in butter and sprinkle on top. Bake in 350° F. oven 30 minutes. Remove from oven and sprinkle with grated cheese. Return to oven for 5 to 8 minutes or until cheese is melted. (If desired, 1 cup drained, flaked, canned tuna or salmon may be added.)

YIELD: *4 servings.*

COTTAGE CHEESE TOMATO-CRAB BAKE

1 can (7¾ ounces) crab meat
1 tablespoon lemon juice
8 ounces elbow macaroni
1 package (8 ounces) cream cheese, softened
½ cup sour cream
½ cup creamed cottage cheese
¼ teaspoon garlic powder
½ teaspoon salt
¼ teaspoon pepper
¼ cup sliced scallions
2 medium tomatoes, sliced thin
1 cup shredded Cheddar cheese

Drain crab meat; sprinkle with lemon juice. Cook macaroni in boiling salted water according to package directions. Drain. Add cream cheese to hot macaroni and toss gently to coat. Add sour cream, cottage cheese, and seasonings. Turn into a shallow buttered 2-quart baking dish. Sprinkle scallions over macaroni. Spread with layer of crab meat, then a layer of sliced tomatoes. Sprinkle tomatoes with additional salt and pepper. Top with shredded cheese. Bake in 350° F. oven 30 minutes.

YIELD: *4 to 6 servings.*

CRAB MEAT AND CLAM CURRY

1 can (7¾ ounces) crab meat
1 can (8 ounces) minced clams, drained
1 to 2 teaspoons curry powder
1 teaspoon lemon juice
2 tablespoons minced onion
¼ cup finely chopped celery
1 can (5 ounces) water chestnuts, drained and chopped
3 cups creamed cottage cheese
Salad greens

Combine all ingredients except salad greens; chill. Serve on salad greens.

YIELD: *4 to 6 servings.*

LOBSTER FONDUE

1 can (10½ ounces) condensed cream of shrimp soup
½ soup can milk
½ cup shredded sharp American cheese
½ cup cooked or canned lobster
Dash paprika
Dash cayenne
2 tablespoons dry sherry, optional

In a chafing dish or saucepan, combine soup and milk. Heat, stirring occasionally. Add cheese, lobster, paprika, and cayenne. Heat until cheese melts, stirring occasionally. Add sherry. Use as an appetizer dunk with large cubes of bread, or pour over toast slices spread with dill butter for a luncheon dish.

YIELD: *3 to 4 servings.*

SWISS FONDUE

1 pound Swiss cheese, shredded
3 tablespoons cornstarch
¼ teaspoon salt
¼ teaspoon white pepper
¼ teaspoon grated nutmeg
2 cups buttermilk
1 clove garlic
1 loaf French bread

Toss Swiss cheese with cornstarch, salt, white pepper, and nutmeg. In a saucepan or chafing dish heat buttermilk with garlic clove over low heat. When hot, remove garlic and add Swiss cheese; stir constantly until cheese is melted. Serve from chafing dish or casserole over a warmer. Each person serves himself from the common dish, dipping chunks of French bread, which are speared on long forks, into cheese sauce.

YIELD: *6 servings.*

BAKED CHEESE FONDUE

3 eggs, separated
1 can (10¾ ounces) condensed cream of chicken or
    mushroom soup
1 cup shredded sharp Cheddar cheese
¼ teaspoon dry mustard
2 cups small bread cubes

Beat egg yolks until thick. Blend in soup, cheese, and mustard; stir in bread cubes. Beat egg whites until stiff, but not dry; fold

into cheese mixture. Spoon into 1½-quart casserole. Bake in
325° F. oven 1 hour.

YIELD: *4 to 6 servings.*

DEVILED EGGS WITH TOMATO RAREBIT

1 can (10¾ ounces) condensed tomato soup
¼ cup milk
½ teaspoon onion juice
1 teaspoon prepared mustard
½ teaspoon Worcestershire sauce
2 cups shredded American cheese
5 eggs, halved and deviled
5 slices toast

Combine soup, milk, onion juice, mustard, and Worcestershire
sauce in saucepan. Heat to serving temperature. Add cheese
and stir until it melts. For each serving, place 2 deviled eggs on
each slice of toast and top each with ¼ cup hot sauce.

YIELD: *5 servings.*

COTTAGE CHEESE SPICED RICE DISH

3 cups cooked rice
¼ cup finely chopped scallions
1½ cups cottage cheese
1 clove garlic, minced
1 cup sour cream
¼ cup milk
¼ teaspoon Tabasco
¼ teaspoon salt
½ cup grated Parmesan cheese

Combine rice and scallions. Blend cottage cheese with garlic,
sour cream, milk, Tabasco, and salt. Stir into rice mixture. Turn

into a greased 1½-quart casserole. Sprinkle with Parmesan cheese. Bake in 350° F. oven 25 minutes.

YIELD: *4 servings.*

CHEESE NOODLE BAKE

1 cup cottage cheese
1 cup wheat germ, divided
1 cup sour cream
¼ cup chopped onion
2 teaspoons Worcestershire sauce
1 teaspoon salt
⅛ teaspoon pepper
½ cup milk
8 ounces medium noodles, cooked
½ cup shredded sharp American cheese

Combine cottage cheese, ½ cup wheat germ, sour cream, onion, seasonings, and milk. Arrange alternate layers of noodles and the cottage cheese mixture in a greased 1½-quart baking dish. Sprinkle remaining wheat germ over top and sprinkle with shredded cheese. Bake in 350° F. oven 45 minutes.

YIELD: *4 servings.*

COTTAGE CHEESE AND SPICED RICE CASSEROLE

3 cups cooked rice
¼ cup finely chopped scallions
1½ cups large curd cottage cheese
1 clove garlic, minced
1 cup sour cream
¼ cup milk
¼ teaspoon Tabasco
½ teaspoon salt
½ cup grated Parmesan cheese

Combine rice and scallions. Combine cottage cheese with garlic, sour cream, milk, Tabasco, and salt. Stir into rice mixture.
Turn into a greased 1½-quart casserole. Sprinkle with Parmesan cheese. Bake in 350° F. oven about 25 minutes.

YIELD: *6 servings.*

TOMATO CHEESE AND EGG RAREBIT

2 cups crushed corn flakes
6 tablespoons melted butter or margarine, divided
¼ cup chopped onion
1 can (10¾ ounces) condensed tomato soup
½ cup milk
2 tablespoons prepared mustard
½ teaspoon salt
⅛ teaspoon pepper
2 cups shredded American cheese
8 hard-cooked eggs, cut in half lengthwise

Mix cereal with 4 tablespoons melted butter. Press half of mixture in an even layer over bottom of 8×8×2-inch baking pan.
Cook onion in remaining 2 tablespoons butter in saucepan
until tender. Add tomato soup, milk, mustard, salt, and pepper.
Heat slowly, stirring constantly. Remove from heat; fold in
cheese. Pour half of mixture into prepared pan. Top with egg
halves. Pour in remaining sauce and sprinkle with cereal mixture. Bake in a 325° F. oven 25 to 30 minutes.

YIELD: *6 servings.*

VEGETABLE-CHEESE BAKE

1 large bunch broccoli or head cauliflower (or 2 [10
ounces each] packages frozen), cooked and
drained

1 can (10¾ ounces) condensed cream of celery, chicken,
    or mushroom soup
⅓ to ½ cup milk
½ cup shredded sharp Cheddar cheese
¼ cup buttered bread crumbs

Place broccoli or cauliflower in shallow 10×6×2-inch baking
dish. Blend soup, milk, and cheese; pour over vegetables. Top
with crumbs. Bake in 350° F. oven 30 minutes or until heated
through.

YIELD: *6 servings.*

CHEESERONI CASSEROLE

8 ounces elbow macaroni
2 cups shredded sharp Cheddar cheese
1 teaspoon salt
¼ teaspoon pepper
¼ teaspoon dried leaf oregano
1 small onion, sliced thin
1 tall can (1⅔ cups) evaporated milk
2 tablespoons grated Parmesan or Romano cheese
1 tomato, cut in 8 wedges

Cook macaroni in boiling salted water according to package
directions. Drain. Place half the macaroni in 2-quart buttered
casserole. Cover with half the Cheddar cheese. Mix salt, pepper, and oregano; sprinkle half over cheese. Separate onion
slices into rings and place half on top of cheese layer. Pour
about half the evaporated milk over onions. Repeat each layer.
Sprinkle Parmesan cheese on top. Bake in 350° F. oven 20
minutes. Place tomato wedges on top of casserole. Return to
oven and continue baking 10 minutes longer.

YIELD: *6 servings.*

COTTAGE CHEESE BLINTZES

1 egg, slightly beaten
1 teaspoon salt
1 cup water
1 cup sifted flour
1 teaspoon butter
2 cups cottage cheese
1 tablespoon sugar
1 teaspoon salt
½ teaspoon ground cinnamon
¼ cup chopped raisins
Grated rind 1 lemon
4 tablespoons butter
Sour cream

Mix egg, salt, and water. Stir in flour and mix until smooth. Melt 1 teaspoon butter in a 6- or 7-inch skillet. Add 2 table-spoonfuls of mix to pan. Cook over low heat until pancake is set but not brown on the bottom. Remove from pan and place on paper towel. Fry remaining batter the same way, using additional butter as needed. Mix cottage cheese, sugar, salt, cinnamon, raisins, and lemon rind until well blended. Place a teaspoonful of cheese filling on each blintz. Fold over and press sides together. Melt 4 tablespoons of butter in a large skillet. Cook the blintzes in the butter until slightly brown on all sides. Serve with sour cream.

YIELD: *4 to 6 servings.*

COTTAGE CHEESE LOBSTER SALAD IN THE SHELL

4 lobsters, about 1 to 1½ pounds each
2 cups creamed cottage cheese

½ *cup sour cream*
¼ *cup chopped stuffed olives*
¼ *cup sliced scallions*
¼ *cup chopped celery*
2 *tablespoons drained capers*
1 *tablespoon finely chopped anchovies*
Parsley

Cook lobsters in boiling salted water to cover 12 minutes per pound. Drain; cool and then chill. Split underside of lobster into halves lengthwise, not cutting all the way through. Open lobster and remove all inedible portions. Remove lobster meat and cube. Mix meat with remaining ingredients. Open lobsters and spoon cottage cheese mixture into the shells. Serve garnished with parsley. Serve with sliced cucumbers, tomatoes, and stuffed olives.

YIELD: *4 servings.*

CHEESE PUFF

3 *cups milk*
½ *cup pastina*
2 *tablespoons butter or margarine*
3 *tablespoons flour*
¾ *cup cubed American cheese*
½ *teaspoon salt*
¼ *teaspoon dry mustard*
2 *eggs, separated*

Heat milk in double boiler. Add pastina and cook 15 minutes, stirring frequently for the first 5 minutes. Blend together butter and flour. Add to pastina mixture and stir gently until thickened. Add cheese and seasonings. Stir until cheese melts. Beat egg yolks and add a little of the hot sauce. Then, stirring constantly, return to double boiler. Beat egg whites until stiff,

but not dry. Fold into pastina mixture. Turn into a greased
1-quart casserole. Bake in 325° F. oven 30 minutes or until
firm.

YIELD: *4 to 6 servings.*

TOP HAT CHEESE AND CORN SOUFFLÉ

¼ cup butter or margarine
¼ cup flour
1 can (1 pound) cream-style corn
⅓ cup milk
¼ teaspoon salt
⅛ teaspoon garlic salt
½ teaspoon Worcestershire sauce
1½ cups shredded Cheddar cheese
½ cup shredded provolone cheese
5 eggs, separated

Melt butter in saucepan; blend in flour. Add corn, milk, salt,
garlic salt, and Worcestershire sauce and cook, stirring constantly, until thickened. Add cheeses and stir until melted.
Blend slightly beaten egg yolks into sauce. Cool slightly. Beat
egg whites until stiff, but not dry. Gently stir one quarter of
the egg whites into cheese sauce. Carefully fold remaining egg
whites into sauce until just blended. Turn into ungreased
2-quart casserole and bake in 350° F. oven 45 to 50 minutes.
Serve immediately.

YIELD: *5 to 6 servings.*

CHEESE-TUNA PUFFS

¼ cup butter or margarine
¼ cup flour
½ teaspoon salt

> *1 tall can (1⅔ cups) evaporated milk*
> *1 cup shredded Cheddar cheese*
> *1 can (6½ or 7 ounces) tuna, drained and flaked*
> *2 eggs, separated*

Melt butter in saucepan; blend in flour and salt. Gradually add evaporated milk and cook, stirring constantly, until mixture thickens and comes to a boil. Stir in Cheddar cheese; heat, stirring constantly, just until cheese melts. Set aside 1¼ cups cheese sauce to serve over baked puffs. Add tuna to remaining cheese mixture. Blend a few tablespoons of hot mixture into egg yolks; return to tuna-cheese sauce. Beat egg whites until stiff, but not dry; fold into tuna mixture. Set custard cups in baking pan; fill cups to top. Pour hot water into pan around cups. Bake in 350° F. oven 30 to 35 minutes. Run spatula around edge of custard cups; invert puffs on serving plate and serve with hot cheese sauce.

YIELD: *4 servings.*

HOT COTTAGE CHEESE PUFF

> *2 tablespoons butter or margarine*
> *¼ cup flour*
> *1 cup milk*
> *4 eggs, separated*
> *½ cup sugar*
> *2 teaspoons grated orange rind*
> *⅓ cup raisins*
> *1 cup creamed cottage cheese, sieved*
> *Fine dry bread crumbs*

Melt butter in saucepan; blend in flour. Gradually add milk and cook, stirring constantly, until mixture thickens and comes to a boil. Cool. Beat in egg yolks, sugar, orange rind, raisins, and cottage cheese. Beat egg whites until stiff, but not dry. Fold egg whites into cheese mixture. Butter a 1½-quart soufflé dish heavily and sprinkle bottom and sides with fine dry bread crumbs. Turn mixture into prepared dish and bake in 350° F. oven 50 to 60 minutes or until top is puffed and richly browned. Serve at once with warm Orange Sauce (below).

ORANGE SAUCE

> 2 tablespoons cornstarch
> ¼ cup sugar
> 2 cups orange juice
> ½ cup slivered toasted almonds

Mix cornstarch with sugar in saucepan. Gradually stir in orange juice. Cook over low heat, stirring constantly, until mixture thickens and clears and comes to a boil. Stir in nuts. Serve warm over soufflé.

ELEGANT CHEESE PUFF

> 1 cup all-purpose flour
> ½ teaspoon salt
> ¼ teaspoon pepper
> 1½ cups sour cream
> 5 tablespoons grated Parmesan cheese, divided
> 5 eggs, separated

Preheat oven to 350° F. Set a 1½-quart well-greased casserole in a shallow baking pan; place in oven. Pour boiling water around casserole to depth of at least 1 inch; let casserole heat while preparing cheese puff. Combine flour, salt, and pepper in a mixing bowl. Blend in sour cream and 4 tablespoons of the Parmesan cheese, until thoroughly combined. Add unbeaten egg yolks; beating until lemon-colored. Beat egg whites until stiff, but not dry. Fold into sour cream mixture, gently but thoroughly. Turn into hot casserole. Sprinkle with remaining tablespoon of Parmesan cheese. Bake until puffy and delicately browned, about 1 hour. Serve immediately with melted butter and additional Parmesan cheese.

YIELD: *4 to 5 servings.*

SOUPER SUNSHINE SOUFFLÉ

1 can (10¾ ounces) condensed cream of mushroom
*   soup*
1 cup shredded American cheese
6 eggs, separated

Preheat oven to 325° F. Set a 2½-quart ungreased casserole in a shallow baking pan; place in oven. Pour boiling water around casserole to depth of at least 1 inch; let casserole heat while soufflé is prepared. Combine mushroom soup and cheese in saucepan; heat thoroughly over low heat until cheese is melted. Beat egg yolks until thick and lemon-colored. Slowly add hot soup mixture to beaten yolks. Beat egg whites until stiff, but not dry. Slowly and gently fold beaten whites into yolk mixture. Turn into hot casserole. To make crown, make shallow path in soufflé about 1 inch from edge with teaspoon. Bake until puffy and delicately browned, about 1 hour. Serve immediately.

YIELD: *5 to 6 servings.*

SOUTHERN SOUFFLÉ

1 quart milk
½ cup butter or margarine
1 cup hominy grits
1 teaspoon salt
3 eggs, separated
1 cup shredded Cheddar cheese

Heat milk and butter over low heat until butter is melted. Slowly add grits and salt to milk, stirring constantly; cook until thickened and bubbly. Slowly add cooked grits to well-beaten yolks, combining thoroughly. Blend in cheese. Beat egg whites until stiff, but not dry. Gently, but thoroughly, fold whites into yolk mixture. Turn into an 11×7-inch ungreased shallow baking dish. Bake in a 350° F. oven until puffy and delicately browned, about 1 hour. Cut in squares and serve immediately topped with Mushroom Sauce (below).

MUSHROOM SAUCE

> *3 tablespoons butter or margarine*
> *3 tablespoons flour*
> *½ teaspoon salt*
> *⅛ teaspoon pepper*
> *1½ cups milk*
> *4 hard-cooked eggs, cut in eighths*
> *2 cans (3 or 4 ounces each) sliced mushrooms, drained*

Melt butter in saucepan, blend in flour, salt, and pepper. Add milk and cook, stirring constantly, until mixture thickens and comes to a boil. Add hard-cooked eggs and drained mushrooms. Heat. Serve hot over squares of soufflé.

YIELD: *6 servings.*

TABASCO CHEESE SOUFFLÉ

> *3 tablespoons butter or margarine*
> *¼ cup flour*
> *1 cup milk*
> *½ teaspoon salt*
> *½ teaspoon Tabasco*

 1 cup shredded sharp Cheddar cheese
 4 eggs, separated
 ¼ teaspoon cream of tartar

Melt butter in saucepan; blend in flour. Gradually add milk, salt, and Tabasco. Cook, stirring constantly, until mixture thickens and comes to a boil. Add cheese to mixture; stir until cheese melts and sauce is smooth. With fork, beat egg yolks. Stir in a little bit of the cheese sauce, then stir this mixture back into the remaining cheese sauce. Do not let mixture boil. Cool slightly. Beat egg whites with cream of tartar until stiff, but not dry; gradually fold in cheese sauce. Turn into ungreased 1½-quart soufflé dish to ¼ inch from top. To make crown, make shallow path in soufflé about 1 inch from edge with teaspoon. Bake in 325° F. oven 55 to 60 minutes until top is golden brown. Meanwhile, prepare Shrimp Sauce (below). Serve soufflé and sauce immediately after removing from oven.

SHRIMP SAUCE

 2 tablespoons butter or margarine
 2 tablespoons flour
 ¼ teaspoon salt
 ¼ teaspoon Tabasco
 ¾ cup milk
 ¼ cup dry sherry
 ½ pound shelled, deveined shrimp, cooked

Melt butter in saucepan; blend in flour, salt, and Tabasco. Gradually add milk and cook, stirring constantly, until mixture thickens and comes to a boil. Add sherry and shrimp, cooking only until shrimp are heated through. Do not boil. Serve with soufflé.

YIELD: *6 servings.*

SUPER CHEESE SOUFFLÉ

1 can (10¾ ounces) condensed cream of celery, chicken,
*   or mushroom soup*
1 cup shredded sharp American cheese
6 eggs, separated

Combine soup and cheese in saucepan; heat slowly until cheese
melts. Beat egg yolks until thick and lemon-colored; stir into
soup mixture. Beat egg whites until stiff, but not dry; fold into
mixture. Turn into ungreased 2-quart casserole. Bake in 300° F.
oven 1 to 1¼ hours, or in 400° F. oven 30 minutes. Serve
immediately.

YIELD: *4 to 6 servings.*

VARIATIONS:

Asparagus Soufflé: Add ⅛ teaspoon ground nutmeg and ½
cup chopped cooked asparagus to cream of mushroom soup-
cheese mixture. Proceed as above.

Mushroom Soufflé: Add ¼ teaspoon chervil, ½ cup finely
minced cooked mushrooms, and 2 tablespoons chopped parsley
to cream of chicken or celery soup-cheese mixture. Proceed
as above.

VEGETABLES

MEATLESS LOAF

1 tablespoon vegetable oil
1 onion, chopped
1 cup cracked wheat, uncooked
2 cups water
2 teaspoons salt, divided
1 pound spinach, cooked (approximately 2 cups)
1 cup unsalted peanuts
2 eggs
½ teaspoon Tabasco

Heat oil in medium saucepan. Add onion and cracked wheat and cook until onion is tender. Add water and ½ teaspoon salt. Bring to boil, cover, reduce heat, and cook over very low heat 15 minutes, until all water is absorbed. Place spinach, peanuts, and eggs in container of electric blender. Cover and process at high speed until puréed and smooth. (It may be necessary to turn the blender on and off at first, pushing contents down with a spatula.) Turn spinach mixture into a large bowl. Stir in cooked cracked wheat, Tabasco, and remaining 1½ teaspoons salt. Turn into a 9×5×3-inch loaf pan that has been lined with well-oiled aluminum foil. Bake in 350° F. oven 55 minutes. Remove from oven and let stand 5 to 10 minutes before removing from pan. Slice with serrated knife for best results. Serve with mayonnaise.

YIELD: *6 servings.*

DOLMADES AMERICAN STYLE

12 large cabbage leaves
½ cup chopped onion
¼ cup melted butter
2 pints oysters, drained
2 cups cooked rice
2 teaspoons salt
½ teaspoon dried leaf basil
2 cups shredded Cheddar cheese
2 cans (8 ounces each) tomato sauce with mushrooms

Parboil cabbage leaves 10 minutes and drain. Cook onion in butter in saucepan until tender. Add oysters and heat until edges curl. Mix rice, salt, basil, and Cheddar cheese together. Blend onion and oysters into cheese-rice mixture. Put about ⅓ cup of this mixture into each cabbage leaf; wrap together and secure with a wooden pick. Place in buttered baking dish and cover with 1 can of the tomato sauce. Bake in 375° F. oven 20 minutes. Heat remaining sauce and serve.

YIELD: 6 servings.

NEAPOLITAN-STYLE EGGPLANT

1 large eggplant
Flour
Salad oil
2 eggs
½ pound mozzarella cheese, cubed
½ pound ricotta cheese
½ cup fine dry bread crumbs
½ teaspoon dried leaf basil

½ *teaspoon salt*
¼ *teaspoon pepper*
1½ *cups Marinara sauce*

Pare and cut eggplant in ¼-inch slices. Dip in flour and fry both sides in salad oil until light brown. Combine eggs, mozzarella and ricotta cheese, bread crumbs, basil, salt, and pepper. Place fried slices of eggplant side by side in shallow baking pan. Spread cheese mixture over each slice of eggplant. Top with another slice of eggplant. Cover with Marinara sauce and sprinkle with grated Parmesan cheese. Bake in a 375° F. oven 25 minutes.

YIELD: *4 servings.*

EGGPLANT À LA BOIARDI

1 large eggplant
1 teaspoon salt
¼ *teaspoon pepper*
½ *cup flour*
1 egg
⅓ *cup shredded Cheddar cheese*
1 cup cracker meal
1 can (8 ounces) tomato sauce, heated

Pare eggplant and cut into ½-inch slices. Season with salt and pepper. Dip slices in flour, then in beaten egg, to which cheese has been added, then in cracker meal. Pat between hands so that eggplant is entirely covered. Fry in small quantity of hot fat until tender and golden brown. Remove from pan to hot platter. Serve with tomato sauce.

YIELD: *4 servings.*

BAKED EGGPLANT PALERMO

2 large eggplants
2 small green bell peppers
2 small tomatoes
1 package (10 ounces) frozen artichoke hearts, cooked
⅓ cup salad oil
½ teaspoon garlic powder
1½ teaspoons dried leaf oregano
1 teaspoon dried leaf basil
2 tablespoons instant minced onion
1 teaspoon salt
1 can (8 ounces) sliced mushrooms, drained
1 cup grated Parmesan cheese, divided

Cut eggplants in half lengthwise; cut ½ inch in from edges all around halves. Scoop out centers of eggplant to form shells. Dice center portion and reserve. Parboil eggplant shells in boiling salted water until just tender, but shape is retained. Drain and place in baking dish. Cut peppers and tomatoes into chunks. Halve artichoke hearts. Cook diced eggplant in salad oil with garlic powder 5 minutes. Stir in oregano, basil, onion, salt, peppers, tomatoes, artichokes, and mushrooms. Simmer 10 minutes until heated through. Stir in ¾ cup Parmesan cheese. Spoon into eggplant shells, filling up quite high. Top with remaining ¼ cup cheese. Bake in 350° F. oven 30 minutes or until heated through.

YIELD: *4 servings.*

BAKED EGGPLANT WITH CHEESE

2 tablespoons butter or margarine
2 tablespoons chopped onion
1 can (6 ounces) tomato paste

1½ cups water
2 teaspoons salt, divided
¼ teaspoon pepper
1 medium eggplant, pared
1 egg, beaten
¼ cup milk
¾ cup fine bread crumbs
½ cup salad oil
1½ cups shredded sharp Cheddar cheese

Melt butter in small saucepan. Add onion and cook until tender. Add tomato paste, water, 1 teaspoon of the salt, and pepper; simmer 5 minutes. Remove from heat. Cut eggplant into ½-inch slices. Mix egg, milk, and remaining 1 teaspoon salt. Dip slices of eggplant into egg mixture, then into crumbs. Heat oil in large skillet and sauté eggplant slices until golden brown. Arrange alternate layers of eggplant, cheese, and tomato sauce in 1½-quart casserole. Top with additional shredded Cheddar cheese and bake in 350° F. oven 30 minutes.

YIELD: *4 servings.*

BAKED EGGPLANT WITH SHRIMP

¼ cup salad oil
½ cup chopped onion
¼ cup diced celery
¼ cup finely chopped green pepper
1 medium eggplant
1 tablespoon flour
1 teaspoon salt
2 chicken bouillon cubes
¾ cup boiling water
¾ cup cooked rice
1 pound shrimp, cleaned, cooked, and deveined
2 tablespoons fine dry bread crumbs
2 teaspoons oil

Heat ¼ cup oil in skillet; add onion, celery, and green pepper and cook slowly 5 minutes. Wash eggplant; cut a lengthwise slice ¾ inch thick from one side. Scoop out pulp to within ¼ inch of skin. Cut pulp into ¾-inch cubes. Blend flour and salt into sautéed vegetables, add cubed eggplant, cover; cook over medium heat, 5 minutes. Dissolve bouillon cubes in boiling water; pour into mixture. Stir in rice and shrimp; heat, stirring occasionally. Mix crumbs with oil. Fill eggplant shell with hot rice-shrimp mixture; sprinkle top with crumbs. Place in shallow baking dish. Bake in 375° F. oven 30 minutes or until thoroughly heated.

YIELD: *4 servings.*

ITALIAN EGGPLANT BAKE

1 medium eggplant, pared and cut in 1- to 1½-inch
    cubes
1 large onion, sliced
1 medium green pepper, sliced
½ small clove garlic, minced
1 teaspoon crushed dried leaf oregano
¼ cup butter or margarine
1 can (10¾ ounces) condensed tomato soup
1 cup water
¼ teaspoon salt
Garlic croutons
Grated Parmesan cheese

Cook eggplant in boiling salted water for 3 minutes; drain and place in 10×6×2-inch baking dish. Cook onion, green pepper, garlic, and oregano in butter in saucepan until tender. Add soup, water, and salt. Heat; pour sauce over eggplant. Bake in 350° F. oven 45 minutes; stir often. Remove eggplant from oven. Turn temperature up to 425° F. Top eggplant with croutons; sprinkle with cheese. Return to oven; bake 15 minutes longer.

YIELD: *6 servings.*

AVOCADO POTATO BOATS

> 2 *avocados*
> 4 *hot baked medium potatoes*
> 2 *teaspoons lemon juice*
> 2 *teaspoons seasoned salt*
> ½ *teaspoon salt*
> ½ *teaspoon seasoned pepper*
> ¼ *cup mayonnaise*

Cut avocados lengthwise into halves; remove seeds and skin. Cut slice from top of each potato; scoop out potato and mash with 1½ avocados. With a fork, whip lemon juice, seasonings, and mayonnaise into potato mixture; spoon into potato shells. Slice remaining avocado half. Garnish potatoes with avocado slices. Broil about 4 inches from heat for a minute or so.

YIELD: *4 servings.*

CAESAR SALAD

SALAD DRESSING:

> ½ *cup salad oil*
> 1 *clove garlic, quartered*
> 1½ *teaspoons salt*
> 1 *teaspoon dry mustard*
> ¾ *teaspoon pepper*
> 3 *tablespoons vinegar*
> 2 *teaspoons Worcestershire sauce*
> ½ *teaspoon sugar*

Combine all ingredients in a jar with a tight-fitting lid. Cover. Shake well and refrigerate at least overnight.

SALAD:

> ½ green pepper, cut in thin strips
> ½ cucumber, peeled and sliced
> 1 small head lettuce
> ½ head endive
> 1 bunch watercress
> 6 radishes, sliced
> 1 cup grated Parmesan cheese
> 1 cup crumbled blue cheese
> 2 cups croutons
> 1 egg
> 1 can (2 ounces) flat fillets anchovies, drained

At serving time combine well-chilled vegetables in a large bowl. Strain garlic from salad dressing and add with cheeses and croutons to greens. Drop in raw egg and toss until well mixed. Garnish with anchovies and serve immediately.

YIELD: 8 to 10 servings.

RED AND WHITE RING SALAD

TOMATO LAYER:

> 1½ cups tomato juice
> ¼ cup finely chopped celery
> 1 tablespoon chopped onion
> ½ teaspoon paprika
> 1 teaspoon salt
> 2 whole cloves
> 1 bay leaf

> 2 *tablespoons sugar*
> 2 *tablespoons lemon juice*
> 1 *envelope unflavored gelatin*
> ½ *cup cold water*

Combine tomato juice, celery, onion, paprika, salt, cloves, bay leaf, sugar, and lemon juice in a saucepan; simmer 10 minutes. Strain; add water to yield 1¾ cups if any juice has evaporated. Sprinkle gelatin on water to soften and add to hot tomato juice; stir until dissolved. Pour into 1½-quart ring mold. Chill until almost firm.

Cottage Cheese Layer:

> 1 *envelope unflavored gelatin*
> 1 *cup cold water, divided*
> 1½ *cups cottage cheese*
> ½ *teaspoon salt*
> ¼ *cup chopped nuts*
> ¼ *cup finely chopped green pepper*
> ½ *cup instant nonfat dry milk*

Sprinkle gelatin on ½ cup of the water to soften; dissolve over hot water. Mix cottage cheese, salt, nuts, green pepper, and dissolved gelatin. Beat nonfat dry milk and remaining ½ cup water until stiff; fold into cottage cheese mixture. Spoon over tomato layer. Chill until firm.

Yield: *6 to 8 servings.*

ARTICHOKES WITH REMOULADE SAUCE

To prepare artichokes, cut 1 inch off the top, cutting straight across with a knife. Cut off stem at base. Pull off outside bottom leaves. Clip off thorny tips on leaves with scissors. Stand artichokes upright in deep saucepan. For each artichoke, add 1 lemon slice. Pour in 1 inch boiling salted water. Boil, uncovered, 5 minutes. Cover and boil 30 to 35 minutes for large artichokes, 15 to 20 minutes for small artichokes, or until a leaf can easily be pulled from stalk. Lift out and drain upside down. Serve with Remoulade Sauce (below).

REMOULADE SAUCE

1 cup mayonnaise
½ teaspoon dry mustard
½ teaspoon garlic salt
1 tablespoon anchovy paste
½ teaspoon Tabasco
2 tablespoons vinegar
1 tablespoon chopped parsley
2 tablespoons chili sauce
3 tablespoons very finely chopped stuffed olives
3 tablespoons very finely chopped gherkins
1 teaspoon very finely chopped onion
3 hard-cooked eggs, very finely chopped

Blend mayonnaise, mustard, garlic salt, anchovy paste, and Tabasco. Stir in vinegar. Add remaining ingredients and mix well. Serve as dunkin' sauce for artichokes.

YIELD: *2 cups.*

SHRIMP AND ARTICHOKE HEARTS

1 package (10 ounces) frozen artichoke hearts,
     cooked
1 can (3 or 4 ounces) sliced mushrooms, drained

1 tablespoon butter or margarine
1 can (10½ ounces) condensed cream of shrimp soup
⅓ cup milk
1 tablespoon dry sherry, optional
1 teaspoon Worcestershire sauce
4 tablespoons grated Parmesan cheese
Paprika

Place artichoke hearts in buttered 1-quart casserole. Brown mushrooms in butter in saucepan; add soup, milk, sherry, and Worcestershire sauce. Heat, stirring occasionally. Pour over artichokes. Top with cheese and sprinkle with paprika. Bake in 375° F. oven 20 minutes.

YIELD: *3 to 4 servings.*

HEARTY BAKED CHEESE TOMATOES

4 large, firm tomatoes
Salt
½ pound Cheddar cheese, cubed
1 cup toasted bread cubes
¼ teaspoon nutmeg
¼ teaspoon salt
1 tablespoon parsley flakes
½ cup chopped cashew nuts
2 tablespoons butter, melted
¼ cup finely chopped onion

Core tomatoes and scoop out insides; dice pulp to make 1 cup; sprinkle lightly with salt. Combine Cheddar cheese, bread cubes, nutmeg, salt, parsley flakes, nuts, butter, onion, and 1 cup tomato pulp. Fill tomatoes with cheese mixture and wrap each in aluminum foil. Bake in 350° F. oven 15 minutes.

YIELD: *4 servings.*

BEAN CHEESE LOAF

1 can (1 pound) kidney beans, drained
½ cup shredded Cheddar cheese
1 onion, chopped
1 tablespoon butter
½ teaspoon salt
⅛ teaspoon pepper
1 cup fine bread crumbs
2 eggs, well beaten
½ cup tomato sauce

Mash kidney beans. Add cheese and blend well. Sauté the onion in the butter for 5 minutes. Add to the bean mixture with the remaining ingredients. Mix thoroughly and pack in well-oiled small loaf pan. Bake in 350° F. oven 30 minutes. This may be served hot or cold, or with additional tomato sauce.

YIELD: *4 servings.*

CHILI CON CARNE

2 tablespoons butter or margarine
1 onion, chopped fine
½ green pepper, chopped fine
1 can (1 pound) red kidney beans, drained
2 to 3 teaspoons chili powder
1 can (8 ounces) tomato sauce

Melt butter in saucepan; add onion and green pepper and cook until tender. Add remaining ingredients; simmer 25 to 30 minutes. Serve hot with crisp salted crackers.

YIELD: *3 servings.*

DANISH EGG SALAD SANDWICH

6 hard-cooked eggs
½ cup finely chopped celery
1 tablespoon finely chopped onion
1 tablespoon vinegar
¼ teaspoon Tabasco
1 teaspoon salt
¼ cup mayonnaise or salad dressing
4 slices white or rye bread
Softened butter or margarine
Lettuce
Pimiento for garnish

Slice 2 hard-cooked eggs and reserve 4 center slices for garnish. Chop all eggs and put in bowl. Add celery and onion to eggs and toss lightly. Stir vinegar, Tabasco, and salt into mayonnaise or salad dressing until well blended. Pour dressing over egg mixture and stir until moistened throughout. Spread each slice of bread with butter; cover bread with lettuce. Scoop egg salad on top of lettuce, dividing it between the 4 sandwiches. Top each with a reserved egg slice and pimiento strips.

YIELD: *4 servings.*

EGG AND TOMATO RAREBIT

6 firm, ripe tomatoes
6 eggs
Garlic salt
Pepper
1 tablespoon melted butter
2 tablespoons bread crumbs
1 teaspoon chopped parsley
½ teaspoon dried leaf basil
1 can (11 ounces) condensed Cheddar cheese soup
¼ teaspoon dry mustard
¼ cup milk
6 slices toast

With a knife, scoop out tomatoes, leaving a ¼-inch shell. Drain. Break eggs into a cup, one at a time, and slip into tomato shells. Place in buttered baking dish. Sprinkle with garlic salt and pepper. Combine butter, bread crumbs, parsley, and basil; sprinkle on eggs. Bake 30 to 35 minutes in 300° F. oven until eggs are of desired consistency. While tomato cups are baking, combine cheese soup, dry mustard, and milk in a small saucepan. Heat over low heat, stirring occasionally, until beginning to boil. Serve over tomato cups on toast.

YIELD: 6 servings.

SALMON WITH VEGETABLES

1 can (8 ounces) salmon
2 tablespoons butter or margarine
2 tablespoons flour
¼ teaspoon curry powder

¼ *teaspoon salt*
¼ *teaspoon onion salt*
Dash pepper
1 small can (⅔ cup) evaporated milk
1 can (8 ounces) peas
1 can (8 ounces) cream-style corn

Drain salmon, reserving liquid; flake salmon coarsely. Melt butter in saucepan; blend in flour, curry powder, salt, onion salt, and pepper. Gradually stir in milk and liquids drained from salmon and peas. Cook, stirring constantly, until mixture thickens and comes to a boil. Add peas, corn, and salmon; heat thoroughly. Spoon over toast, crackers, or heated chow mein noodles.

YIELD: *4 servings.*

SALMON BROCCOLI PIE

1 can (1 pound) salmon
Milk
¼ *cup butter or margarine*
¼ *cup flour*
½ *teaspoon dried leaf thyme*
¼ *teaspoon pepper*
1 can (3 or 4 ounces) chopped mushrooms, drained
1 tablespoon chopped parsley
1½ *cups cooked, drained, chopped broccoli*
1 cup pastry mix

Drain salmon, reserving liquid. Add enough milk to salmon liquid to make 2 cups. Break salmon into large pieces. Melt butter in saucepan; blend in flour and seasonings. Gradually add milk mixture and cook, stirring constantly, until mixture thickens and comes to a boil. Add mushrooms, parsley, and salmon. Spread broccoli in a 9-inch pie pan. Pour salmon mixture over broccoli. Prepare pastry mix as directed. Roll dough to form a 10-inch circle. Place dough over salmon mixture. Double edge of pastry over and pinch with fingers to make an upright rim. Cut top to allow steam to escape. Bake in 425° F. oven 20 to 25 minutes or until brown.

YIELD: *6 servings.*

CRAB MEAT STUFFED SQUASH SUPREME

4 small acorn squash
6 tablespoons melted butter or margarine, divided
¼ cup chopped onion
3 cups soft bread cubes
1 can (7¾ ounces) crab meat, flaked
¼ cup chopped stuffed olives
1 tablespoon lemon juice
1 egg, beaten

Cut squash in half lengthwise. Remove seeds, and place cut side down in baking pan with 4 tablespoons of the melted butter. Bake in 350° F. oven 30 minutes. Cook onion in remaining 2 tablespoons butter until tender. Combine with soft bread cubes, crab meat, olives, lemon juice, and beaten egg; mix well. Remove squash from oven, turn, brush inside with butter from pan. Fill each with about ⅓ cup stuffing mixture. Bake 30 minutes longer.

YIELD: *8 servings.*

ASPARAGUS SUPPER CASSEROLE

1 package (10 ounces) frozen asparagus
4 hard-cooked eggs, sliced

> ¼ *cup butter or margarine*
> ¼ *cup flour*
> 1½ *cups milk*
> ½ *cup dry sauterne*
> ¾ *teaspoon seasoned salt*
> 3 *tablespoons chopped chives*
> ½ *cup grated Cheddar cheese*
> 1 *large tomato*
> ¼ *cup fine dry bread crumbs*
> 1 *tablespoon melted butter*

Cook asparagus; drain and cut into bite-size pieces. Place in a 1½-quart casserole. Top with egg slices. Melt ¼ cup butter in saucepan; blend in flour. Gradually add milk and cook, stirring constantly, until mixture thickens and comes to a boil. Blend in wine, salt, chives, and cheese. Pour over asparagus. Cut tomato into thin slices and arrange over sauce; sprinkle with bread crumbs mixed with the butter. Bake in 375° F. oven 25 to 30 minutes.

YIELD: *4 servings.*

CELERY AND COTTAGE CHEESE-STUFFED TOMATOES

> 1½ *cups cottage cheese*
> 3 *tablespoons chopped chives*
> ¼ *teaspoon salt*
> ⅛ *teaspoon pepper*
> 6 *large tomatoes*
> 1½ *cups sliced celery*
> *Salad greens*

Combine cottage cheese, chives, salt, and pepper. Set aside. Divide each tomato into eighths, cutting them three quarters of the way through, being sure not to break the tomatoes apart. Sprinkle with salt and pepper. Spoon cottage cheese mixture in center of each. Top with sliced celery. Place on salad greens and serve with Lemon French Dressing (below).

YIELD: *6 servings.*

LEMON FRENCH DRESSING

> *1 cup salad oil*
> *½ teaspoon salt or salt to taste*
> *½ teaspoon dry mustard*
> *⅛ teaspoon pepper*
> *1 teaspoon sugar*
> *1 clove garlic, peeled and split*
> *2 teaspoons minced onion*
> *3 tablespoons lemon juice*
> *2 tablespoons cider vinegar*
> *1 egg white*

Combine first 7 ingredients and let stand 1 hour. Remove garlic. Add lemon juice, vinegar, and egg white. Beat with a rotary beater until thickened. Chill and serve over vegetable or fruit salads.

EASY TIME CASSEROLE WITH CEREAL TOPPING

> *1 can (10½ ounces) condensed cream of celery soup*
> *¼ teaspoon dried leaf marjoram*
> *¾ cup milk*
> *1 package (9 ounces) frozen green beans, cooked*
> *3 hard-cooked eggs, coarsely chopped*
> *1 cup shredded Cheddar cheese*
> *1½ cups crushed shredded rice or corn, bite-size biscuits*

Mix together soup, marjoram, and milk. Stir in beans, eggs, and cheese. Blend ¾ cup of crushed shredded rice or corn into mixture. Turn into greased 1-quart casserole and top with remaining cereal. Bake in 350° F. oven 40 minutes or until heated through.

YIELD: *4 servings.*

EGG-STUFFED AVOCADO

2 large avocados
2 tablespoons lemon juice
½ cup finely chopped celery
⅓ cup soft bread crumbs
¼ cup milk
½ teaspoon grated lemon peel
½ teaspoon salt
¼ teaspoon pepper
⅛ teaspoon powdered ginger
6 hard-cooked eggs, chopped
¼ cup soft bread crumbs, buttered

Cut avocados in half lengthwise; remove seeds. Scoop out most of pulp to make a nest for the filling. Brush avocado with lemon juice. Mash the avocado pulp and combine with celery, bread crumbs, milk, lemon peel, and seasonings, blending well. Gently add chopped hard-cooked eggs. Fill avocados with egg salad mixture. Top each avocado half with buttered crumbs. Bake in a 400° F. oven until crumbs are lightly browned and salad hot, about 15 to 20 minutes. Serve at once.

YIELD: *4 servings.*

FRESH VEGETABLE RAREBIT

2 tablespoons butter or margarine
2 tablespoons flour
⅓ teaspoon salt
Dash cayenne
¼ teaspoon dry mustard
½ teaspoon Worcestershire sauce
1 cup milk
1½ cups grated American cheese
½ cup chopped cooked celery
¾ cup chopped cooked carrots
¾ cup cooked peas
8 slices toast

Melt butter in saucepan. Blend in flour, salt, pepper, mustard, and Worcestershire sauce. Gradually add milk and cook, stirring constantly, until mixture thickens and comes to a boil. Add cheese and stir until cheese melts. Add celery, carrots, and peas; heat to serving temperature. Serve on toast.

YIELD: *8 servings.*

COTTAGE POTATO ESCALLOP

4 tablespoons butter or margarine, divided
3 tablespoons flour
½ cup milk
⅛ teaspoon salt
⅛ teaspoon pepper
¼ teaspoon rosemary
2 teaspoons grated onion
1½ cups cottage cheese
4 medium potatoes, boiled and thinly sliced

Melt 3 tablespoons of the butter in a saucepan. Blend in flour; add milk. Stir vigorously over moderate heat. Continue to cook until sauce thickens, stirring constantly. Remove from heat. Stir in salt, pepper, rosemary, onion, and cheese. Cook over low heat, stirring constantly, until curds disappear and sauce becomes thin. Alternate layers of potatoes and sauce in a buttered 2-quart casserole. Dot with remaining tablespoon butter. Bake in 350° F. oven 1 hour.

YIELD: *6 servings.*

STUFFED PEPPERS SUPREME

4 medium green peppers
1 onion, finely chopped
1 clove garlic, minced
2 tablespoons minced parsley
1 cup cooked rice
1 cup fine bread crumbs
2 tablespoons butter
1½ cups Marinara sauce

Cut the top off the peppers around the stem and remove the seeds and membrane. Cover pepper shells with boiling water and let stand 5 minutes. Drain. Combine the onion, garlic, parsley, rice, bread crumbs, and butter. Fill pepper shells with this mixture. Place in a casserole and pour the sauce around them. Cover and bake in 350° F. oven 30 minutes.

YIELD: *4 servings.*

SHRIMP AND CRAB-STUFFED POTATOES

1 can (10½ ounces) condensed cream of shrimp soup
¼ cup milk
1 tablespoon grated onion
Dash pepper
½ cup shredded sharp Cheddar cheese
4 medium baking potatoes, baked
1 can (7¾ ounces) crab meat
Paprika

Combine soup, milk, onion, and pepper in saucepan. Heat, stirring occasionally. Add cheese; stir until melted. Cut potatoes in half lengthwise. Scoop out insides; place in bowl. Add soup mixture slowly; mix until blended and fluffy. Fold in crab meat. Spoon into potato shells. Bake on cookie sheet in a 450° F. oven 15 minutes. Sprinkle with paprika.

YIELD: *4 servings.*

ORIENTAL STUFFED CABBAGE

1 large head green cabbage
2½ quarts boiling water
2 tablespoons finely chopped onion
2 tablespoons melted butter
¼ teaspoon salt
2¼ cups cooked rice
¼ to ½ teaspoon dried leaf thyme
1 teaspoon Worcestershire sauce
1 cup cottage cheese
1 can (8 ounces) tomato sauce
⅛ teaspoon pepper
12 broiled apple slices

Trim off outer leaves and stem of cabbage. Cook whole cabbage in boiling salted water until almost tender. Drain well. Cut thin slice from base to stand cabbage. Scoop out enough of inside to leave about 1½-inch shell. Reserve cabbage leaves for garnish. Stand cabbage in a greased shallow casserole; keep hot. Brown onion in butter in saucepan. Add salt and remaining ingredients except apple slices; mix well and heat thoroughly, stirring constantly. Pack mixture into cabbage shell. Bake in 400° F. oven 10 to 15 minutes. Serve garnished with cabbage leaves and apple slices.

YIELD: *4 to 6 servings.*

MUSHROOM-STUFFED TOMATOES

8 large firm tomatoes
¼ cup finely chopped onion
¼ cup finely chopped celery
3 tablespoons melted butter or margarine
1 quart toasted bread cubes
1 can (10¾ ounces) condensed cream of mushroom
    soup
¼ cup grated Parmesan cheese

Slice off top of tomatoes and scoop out the centers; place in a greased baking dish. Brown onion and celery in butter. Add to toasted bread cubes with undiluted soup; mix well. Stuff mixture into tomato shells. Sprinkle cheese over top of each tomato. Bake in 350° F. oven 30 minutes.

YIELD: *8 servings.*

SALADS

HEARTY SUPPER SALAD

1 cup elbow macaroni
2 cups diced cooked shrimp
1½ cups diced sharp Cheddar cheese
1 cup sliced celery
1 small onion, chopped
½ cup chopped sweet pickle
½ cup sour cream
2 tablespoons prepared mustard

Cook macaroni in boiling salted water until tender, according to package directions. Drain and chill. Put in mixing bowl with shrimp, Cheddar cheese, celery, onion, and pickle. Blend together sour cream and mustard. Add to macaroni mixture. Toss until well blended. Chill thoroughly before serving.

YIELD: *6 servings.*

SHRIMP SALAD BOWL WITH REMOULADE SAUCE

1 pound shrimp
1 teaspoon pickling spices
1 quart boiling water
Salad greens
9 ripe olives
3 hard-cooked eggs, quartered
2 tomatoes, cut in wedges

Cook shrimp with pickling spices 5 minutes in a quart of boiling water. Chill shrimp, then shell and devein. At serving time, make a bed of salad greens in each individual salad bowl. Place 6 shrimp, 3 olives, and several egg and tomato wedges in an attractive arrangement on top of each. Top with Remoulade Sauce (below).

YIELD: *3 servings.*

REMOULADE SAUCE

¾ cup mayonnaise
¼ cup prepared mustard
⅛ teaspoon garlic salt
¼ cup minced onion
⅛ teaspoon sugar
Salt
Pepper
½ teaspoon prepared horseradish
¼ teaspoon celery seed
1 teaspoon Worcestershire sauce
1 tablespoon lemon juice
1 tablespoon capers

Mix all ingredients together. Garnish, if desired, with additional capers. Serve over chilled shrimp salad.

YIELD: 1¼ cups.

GOURMET EGG LOUIS

1 quart torn salad greens
9 hard-cooked eggs, cut in quarters
1 avocado, peeled, pitted, and cut in lengthwise slices
2 medium tomatoes, cut in wedges
½ teaspoon salt

Place greens in large salad bowl; toss. Arrange hard-cooked eggs in center of bowl on top of greens. Alternate avocado slices with tomato wedges around edge. Sprinkle all with salt and serve with Gourmet Egg Louis Dressing (below).

YIELD: 4 to 6 servings.

GOURMET EGG LOUIS DRESSING

1 cup mayonnaise or salad dressing
¼ cup chili sauce
1 hard-cooked egg, finely chopped
2 tablespoons finely chopped ripe olives
2 teaspoons chopped chives
1 teaspoon lemon juice

Combine all ingredients; chill.

YIELD: *1½ cups.*

MOUSSE DE SAUMON

1 can (1 pound) salmon
1 envelope unflavored gelatin
½ cup cold water
1 cup mayonnaise
⅓ cup red wine vinegar
¼ teaspoon salt
½ teaspoon dried dillweed
1 tablespoon capers
⅛ teaspoon Tabasco
½ pint sour cream
Crisp salad greens

Drain salmon well; remove skin and bones. Sprinkle gelatin on cold water to soften. Place over low heat; stir until dissolved. Gradually stir into mayonnaise. Add red wine vinegar, salt, dill, capers, and Tabasco. Chill until mixture mounds when dropped from a spoon. Fold in sour cream and salmon. Turn into a 1½-quart mold. Chill until firm. Unmold on crisp salad greens.

YIELD: *10 servings.*

KING-OF-THE-SEA SALAD

2 pounds halibut, cooked, boned, and flaked†
1 cucumber, peeled, quartered, and sliced
1 cup sliced celery
½ cup pickle relish
2 tablespoons capers
2 hard-cooked eggs, sliced
1 cup mayonnaise or salad dressing
Lettuce leaves

Combine halibut, cucumber, celery, pickle relish, capers, and hard-cooked eggs. Toss lightly with mayonnaise or salad dressing. Serve on lettuce leaves.

YIELD: *8 servings.*

† To cook the halibut, bring 2 quarts water to boil with 2 teaspoons mixed pickling spices and 2 teaspoons salt. Reduce heat. Add halibut and simmer until fish is done, about 6 to 8 minutes. Lift out fish with slotted spatula. Drain. Chill. When ready to prepare salad, remove skin and bones and flake with a fork.

SEAFOOD SALAD

2 cups cooked crab meat, shrimp, or lobster
½ cup diced celery
2 tablespoons minced onion
½ cup cooked peas
2 tablespoons chopped sweet pickle
3 hard-cooked eggs, diced
Salt to taste
½ cup mayonnaise
Lettuce leaves

Combine ingredients except lettuce; mix lightly. Chill. Serve on lettuce, garnished with additional mayonnaise and sliced hard-cooked eggs, or sliced stuffed olives.

YIELD: *6 servings.*

SEASHORE SALAD

1 envelope unflavored gelatin
½ cup cold water
1 can (10½ ounces) condensed cream of shrimp soup
1 package (3 ounces) cream cheese, softened
1 cup minced celery
1 can (7¾ ounces) crab meat
2 tablespoons chopped parsley
1 teaspoon grated lemon rind
Salad greens

Sprinkle gelatin on cold water to soften. Place over low heat; stir until gelatin is dissolved. Remove from heat. Blend soup with cream cheese; stir in gelatin and remaining ingredients except salad greens. Chill until mixture mounds when dropped from a spoon. Turn into 1½-quart mold. Chill until firm. Unmold; serve on crisp salad greens.

YIELD: *6 servings.*

CALICO CRAB SALAD

2 cups crab meat
1 cup sliced celery
1 cup diced green pepper
¼ cup coarsely chopped pimiento
1 can (13½ ounces) pineapple tidbits
½ cup mayonnaise
½ teaspoon dried dillweed
1 tablespoon lemon juice
Salad greens

Combine crab meat, celery, green pepper, and pimiento in a large bowl. Drain pineapple, reserving 2 tablespoons syrup. Blend reserved pineapple syrup with mayonnaise, dillweed,

and lemon juice. Add to crab mixture with drained pineapple
tidbits. Toss lightly. Chill well. Spoon onto crisp salad greens
to serve.

YIELD: *4 servings.*

CREAMY TUNA MOLD

> *1 envelope unflavored gelatin*
> *½ cup cold water*
> *1 can (10½ ounces) condensed cream of celery soup*
> *1 package (3 ounces) cream cheese, softened*
> *1 can (6½ or 7 ounces) tuna, drained and flaked*
> *½ cup shredded carrots*
> *⅓ cup chopped celery*
> *2 tablespoons chopped parsley*
> *1 tablespoon lemon juice*
> *Salad greens*

Sprinkle gelatin on cold water to soften. Place over low heat;
stir until gelatin is dissolved. Remove from heat. Blend soup
with cream cheese; stir in gelatin and remaining ingredients
except salad greens. Chill until mixture mounds when dropped
from a spoon. Turn into 1-quart mold. Chill until firm. Unmold; serve on crisp salad greens.

YIELD: *4 servings.*

PARTY TUNA-PINEAPPLE SALAD

> *1 cup mayonnaise*
> *2 teaspoons curry powder*
> *½ teaspoon salt*
> *1 cup diagonally cut celery*

    2 cups cooked rice
    1 can (20 ounces) pineapple tidbits, drained
    3 cans (6½ or 7 ounces each) tuna, drained and
        flaked
    Salad greens
    Slivered almonds

Combine mayonnaise, curry powder, and salt. Toss with celery, rice, pineapple tidbits, and tuna. Chill. To serve, arrange on salad greens; garnish with slivered almonds.

YIELD: *6 servings.*

TUNA-ASPARAGUS SALAD

    3 cans (6½ or 7 ounces each) tuna, drained
    1 cup diced celery
    ½ cup sliced pitted ripe olives
    2 pounds asparagus, cooked and chilled
    ¾ teaspoon salt
    ⅓ cup mayonnaise
    ⅓ cup sour cream
    2 tablespoons lemon juice
    1 tablespoon minced onion
    1 teaspoon sugar
    ½ teaspoon dried dillweed
    ½ teaspoon Tabasco
    Salad greens
    Cherry tomatoes or tomato wedges

Break tuna into pieces; place in large bowl with celery and ripe olives. Reserve half of asparagus; cut remaining into 1-inch pieces and add to tuna mixture. Sprinkle salt over salad. Combine mayonnaise and sour cream; stir in lemon juice, onion, sugar, dill, and Tabasco. Add to tuna-asparagus mixture and toss lightly. Chill. At serving time, mound salad in center of platter. Garnish with salad greens, reserved asparagus spears, and cherry tomatoes.

YIELD: *6 servings.*

TUNA PARTY SALAD PLATTER

3 carrots, pared, cut in julienne strips, and
    cooked
½ head cauliflower, broken into flowerets and cooked
1 cup French dressing
3 cans (6½ or 7 ounces each) tuna, drained and broken
    into pieces
Lettuce
1 small cucumber, scored and thinly sliced
½ pint cherry tomatoes
1 can (1 pound) whole green beans, drained
3 slices lemon

Marinate carrots and cauliflower in dressing several hours. Place tuna in the center of serving platter and surround with lettuce cups. Drain carrots and cauliflower and arrange with remaining vegetables on lettuce. Top tuna with lemon slices. Serve with dressing.

YIELD: *6 servings.*

PRETTY-AS-A-PICTURE TUNA SALAD

8 ounces bow-shaped macaroni, cooked according to
    package directions
1 small red onion, sliced and separated into rings
1 cup diagonally sliced celery

  1 cup carrot flowers‡
  3 cans (6½ or 7 ounces each) tuna, drained and broken
   into pieces
  1 cup mayonnaise
  ¼ cup French dressing
  ½ teaspoon salt
  ¼ teaspoon Tabasco
  Salad greens

Combine cooked macaroni, vegetables, and tuna; reserve. Combine remaining ingredients except salad greens. Pour over reserved macaroni-tuna mixture; toss together lightly. Line salad bowl with salad greens; add macaroni-tuna mixture.

YIELD: *6 to 8 servings.*

‡ *To make carrot flowers, cut 1 cup thin carrot slices. Form flower petals by cutting 5 small wedge-shaped notches around the edge of each carrot slice.*

SALMON BUFFET

  3 cans (8 ounces each) salmon, chilled
  1 head endive
  3 slices lemon
  Capers
  3 hard-cooked eggs, quartered
  1 cucumber, peeled and sliced crosswise
  6 cauliflower flowerets
  6 ripe olives
  1 carrot, cut into strips

Drain salmon, being careful not to break cylindrical shape. Separate and wash endive. Arrange on a serving platter. Place the 3 salmon cylinders in a row in the center of the platter. Garnish salmon with lemon slices and capers. Arrange remaining ingredients around salmon.

YIELD: *6 servings.*

CHILLED SALMON WITH CUCUMBER SAUCE

> *1 can (1 pound) salmon, chilled and drained*
> *4 hard-cooked eggs, sliced*
> *Watercress or lettuce*
> *¼ cup heavy cream*
> *¼ cup mayonnaise or salad dressing*
> *¼ cup coarsely chopped peeled cucumber*
> *2 teaspoons chopped chives or onion*
> *1 teaspoon lemon juice or vinegar*

Divide salmon into 4 portions. Arrange salmon and hard-cooked eggs on bed of watercress or lettuce. Combine remaining ingredients; spoon over salad.

YIELD: *4 servings.*

SALMON LUNCHEON SALAD

> *¼ cup French dressing*
> *1½ tablespoons lemon juice or vinegar*
> *1½ teaspoons capers*
> *¼ teaspoon salt*
> *Dash pepper*
> *1 can (1 pound) salmon, drained and flaked*
> *1 can (8 ounces) peas, drained*
> *½ cucumber, peeled and sliced*
> *3 hard-cooked eggs, sliced*
> *Lettuce or watercress*

Combine French dressing, lemon juice, capers, salt, and pepper. Add salmon, peas, cucumber, and eggs; toss lightly; cover and chill. Serve on crisp greens.

YIELD: *4 servings.*

SALMON FRUIT SALAD

1 can (1 pound) salmon, drained
1 tablespoon lemon juice
2 oranges, peeled and sectioned
1 banana, sliced
1 unpared red-skinned apple, diced
¼ cup toasted slivered almonds
3 cups torn lettuce leaves
¼ cup mayonnaise or salad dressing

Break salmon into pieces and sprinkle with lemon juice. Combine orange sections, banana, and apple. Add salmon, almonds, lettuce, and mayonnaise or salad dressing. Toss ingredients together lightly. Serve immediately.

YIELD: *6 servings.*

SALMON MARINADE

1 cup sour cream
1 onion, thinly sliced
3 slices lemon
1 tablespoon lemon juice
8 whole cloves
8 whole peppercorns
3 whole allspice
2 bay leaves
½ teaspoon salt
1 can (1 pound) salmon, drained and flaked
Lettuce or watercress

Combine all ingredients except salmon and salad greens; pour over salmon. Cover; chill 2 hours to blend flavors. Remove whole spices and bay leaves. Serve on crisp lettuce or watercress.

YIELD: *4 servings.*

SALMON SOUFFLÉ SALAD

> *1 package (3 ounces) lemon-flavored gelatin*
> *1 cup hot water*
> *½ cup cold water*
> *3 tablespoons vinegar*
> *½ cup mayonnaise*
> *¼ teaspoon salt*
> *Dash pepper*
> *1 can (1 pound) salmon, drained and flaked*
> *1 cup minced celery*
> *4 tablespoons finely chopped parsley*
> *1½ tablespoons minced onion*
> *Salad greens*

Dissolve gelatin in hot water. Add cold water, vinegar, mayonnaise, salt, and pepper; blend well with rotary beater. Pour into refrigerator tray; chill in freezer 15 to 20 minutes, or until firm around edge but soft in center. Turn mixture into bowl; whip with rotary beater until fluffy. Fold in remaining ingredients except salad greens. Turn into a 1-quart mold or 6 individual molds. Chill until firm. Unmold and garnish with crisp salad greens.

YIELD: *6 servings.*

FISH

BAKED STUFFED FILLETS

2 *fish fillets, about 1 pound each*
1 *teaspoon salt*
⅛ *teaspoon pepper*
4 *tablespoons melted butter or margarine*

Sprinkle both sides of the fish with salt and pepper. Place 1 fillet in well-greased baking pan. Place Herb Stuffing (below) on fish; cover with remaining fillet. Fasten together with toothpicks or skewers. Brush top with melted butter. Bake in a 350° F. oven 30 to 40 minutes or until fish flakes easily when tested with fork.

YIELD: *4 to 6 servings.*

HERB STUFFING

3 *tablespoons melted butter or margarine*
2 *tablespoons chopped onion*
⅓ *cup chopped celery*
½ *teaspoon salt*
⅛ *teaspoon pepper*
½ *teaspoon dried leaf thyme, sage, or savory*
2 *cups day-old bread crumbs*
2 *tablespoons water or milk, optional*

Melt butter in saucepan; add onion and celery and cook until tender. Add with seasonings to bread crumbs; mix well. If too dry, add 2 tablespoons water or milk.

BUBBLING FISH BAKE

2 tablespoons butter or margarine
¼ cup chopped onion
1 can (10 ounces) condensed cream of asparagus soup
½ cup milk
1 cup shredded sharp Cheddar cheese, divided
2 cups cooked macaroni or noodles
1 can (8 ounces) salmon, drained
4 tablespoons buttered bread crumbs

Melt butter in saucepan; add onion and cook until tender. Stir in soup, milk, ¾ cup cheese, macaroni, and salmon. Turn into a 1½-quart casserole. Top with bread crumbs and remaining cheese. Bake in a 350° F. oven 30 minutes.

YIELD: *4 servings.*

SAUCY FISH FILLETS

1 pound fish fillets
1 can (10½ ounces) condensed cream of celery soup
¼ cup milk
1 cup shredded Cheddar cheese
2 tablespoons chopped parsley

Arrange fillets in a 10×6×2-inch baking dish. Blend together soup and milk; spoon over fish. Sprinkle with cheese and top with parsley. Bake in a 400° F. oven 20 minutes.

YIELD: *4 servings.*

GROUNDFISH MAINE STYLE

1½ cups flaked cooked whitefish
2 hard-cooked eggs; chop yolks and whites separately
¼ teaspoon paprika
⅛ teaspoon celery salt
Salt
3 tablespoons butter or margarine
1 package (12 ounces) frozen rice pilaf with mushrooms
*   and onions*
Parsley

Combine flaked fish, chopped egg whites, and seasonings. Heat in butter, stirring occasionally. Prepare rice pilaf according to package directions. Place pilaf on platter and top with fish mixture and garnish with sieved egg yolks and parsley.

YIELD: *4 servings.*

FISH CUTLETS OREGANO

1 tablespoon butter or margarine
1 tablespoon flour
1 can (1 pound, 4 ounces) tomatoes
½ teaspoon salt
¼ teaspoon pepper
1 teaspoon dried leaf oregano
2 packages (8 ounces each) breaded frozen fish
*   portions (fillets, cutlets, burgers, or steaks)*

Melt butter in saucepan; blend in flour. Add tomatoes, salt, pepper, and oregano. Cook over medium heat 5 minutes. Pour over fish portions in individual shallow baking dish. Bake according to package directions.

YIELD: 4 servings.

FRUITED FILLETS

> ¼ cup butter or margarine
> ¼ cup chopped onion
> ⅓ cup chopped celery
> 1 quart toasted bread cubes
> 1 cup diced fresh grapefruit sections
> 1 tablespoon minced parsley
> 1 teaspoon salt
> ½ teaspoon poultry seasoning
> ⅛ teaspoon pepper
> ¼ cup grapefruit juice
> 6 perch or pike fillets

Melt butter in saucepan. Add onion and celery; cook until tender. Combine with toasted bread cubes, grapefruit sections, parsley, salt, poultry seasoning, and pepper. Add grapefruit juice and mix well. Line 6 well-greased muffin cups with fish fillets, placing skin side toward inside of pan. Place ⅓ cup stuffing in the center of each fillet. Bake in a 350° F. oven 30 minutes.

YIELD: 3 servings.

KEDGEREE

> 1 cup uncooked rice
> 2 tablespoons butter
> 1 medium onion
> 2 cups flaked cooked fish
> 1 teaspoon salt

> *Dash pepper*
> *1 pimiento, diced*
> *2 tablespoons chopped parsley*
> *2 teaspoons curry powder*
> *1 hard-cooked egg, chopped*
> *1 hard-cooked egg, sliced*

Cook rice according to package directions; reserve. Melt butter in saucepan; add onion and cook until tender. Remove from heat; add fish, rice, salt, pepper, pimiento, chopped parsley, curry powder, and chopped egg; toss gently to mix well. Heat in double boiler, or in greased casserole in 350° F. oven 15 to 20 minutes or until heated through. Garnish with sliced egg and parsley.

YIELD: *6 servings.*

BOUILLABAISSE

> *4 tablespoons butter or margarine*
> *1 medium carrot, sliced*
> *2 medium onions, sliced*
> *1 clove garlic*
> *3 pounds fish, cooked and boned (cod, whiting,*
>   *haddock, halibut, etc.)*
> *1 cup tomatoes*
> *1 bay leaf*
> *2 cups fish stock or water*
> *1 dozen oysters, clams, or scallops*
> *1 cup shrimp or crab meat*
> *2 teaspoons salt*
> *½ teaspoon pepper*
> *2 tablespoons lemon juice*
> *¼ cup dry sherry*

Melt butter in a very large saucepan. Add carrot, onions, and garlic; cook 10 minutes and remove garlic. Add fish, tomatoes, bay leaf, and stock. Simmer 15 minutes. Remove bay leaf; add remaining ingredients, except sherry. Cook 5 minutes longer. Add sherry; serve immediately.

YIELD: *6 to 8 servings.*

PLANKED FISH

1 (3- or 4-pound) whole fish, dressed
1½ teaspoons salt
⅛ teaspoon pepper
4 tablespoons melted butter or margarine
Seasoned mashed potatoes
Seasoned cooked vegetables (peas, cauliflower,
      tomatoes, green beans, or onions)
Parsley
Lemon wedges

If hardwood plank is used, oil well and place in cold oven to heat while oven preheats. Clean, wash, and dry fish. Sprinkle inside and out with salt and pepper. Brush with melted butter. Place fish on plank or greased ovenproof platter. Bake in a moderate 350° F. oven, 12 minutes per pound, until fish flakes easily when tested with fork. Remove from oven; quickly arrange border of hot mashed potatoes around fish. Place under broiler heat to brown potatoes lightly, about 5 minutes. Remove; arrange 2 or more hot vegetables around fish. Garnish with parsley and lemon wedges.

YIELD: *6 servings.*

FRENCH FRIED FISH

2 pounds fish fillets
1 egg, beaten

2 tablespoons milk
½ cup corn meal
Oil for deep-frying
Salt
Parsley
Lemon slices or wedges
Tartar sauce, optional

Cut fish into serving pieces. Combine egg and milk. Dip fillets into egg mixture first, then into corn meal. Allow to dry, about 5 minutes. Deep-fry in oil heated to 350° F. for 2 to 3 minutes or until golden brown. Do not overcook. Drain on absorbent paper; sprinkle with salt. Garnish with parsley and lemon; serve with tartar sauce, if desired.

YIELD: *6 to 8 servings.*

BARBECUE-BAKED FISH

1 pound fish fillets
Salt
Pepper
1 tablespoon butter or margarine
4 thin slices lemon
4 thin onion rings
2 tablespoons chopped parsley
1 can (10¾ ounces) condensed tomato soup
¼ cup water

Place fillets in a 10×6×2-inch baking dish. Sprinkle with salt and pepper; dot with butter. Top with lemon, onion, and parsley. Combine soup and water; pour over fish. Bake in a 350° F. oven 25 minutes.

YIELD: *4 servings.*

FRIED FISH FILLETS

1 egg
½ cup milk
1 pound fish fillets
¾ cup flour
3 tablespoons sesame seeds
2 teaspoons salt
Oil for deep-frying

Beat egg and milk together until blended. Dip fillets into milk mixture and then in mixture of flour, sesame seeds, and salt. Deep-fry in oil heated to 375° F. for 2 to 3 minutes or until golden brown.

YIELD: *3 to 4 servings.*

FISH STICKS WITH MOCK HOLLANDAISE

1 package (10 ounces) frozen fish sticks
1 package (10 ounces) frozen cut green beans
¾ cup sour cream, divided
1 egg yolk
2 tablespoons lemon juice
¼ teaspoon salt

Cook fish sticks and green beans separately according to individual package directions. While fish and beans are cooking, combine ¼ cup of the sour cream with egg yolk, lemon juice, and salt in saucepan. Cook over low heat, stirring constantly, until thickened. Remove from heat; stir in remaining sour cream. Drain green beans; place in serving dish, top with fish sticks. Pour sauce over all.

YIELD: *3 to 4 servings.*

DILLY FISH

> 2 *pounds fish fillets*
> *Salt*
> *Pepper*
> ½ *cup butter or margarine, divided*
> 1 *tablespoon chopped parsley*
> 1 *tablespoon chopped fresh dill or 1 teaspoon dried*
>   *dillweed*
> *Lemon wedges*

Cut fillets into serving-size pieces. Sprinkle both sides with salt and pepper. Melt half the butter and let the remaining butter soften at room temperature. Preheat broiler 10 minutes. Place pieces of fish on aluminum foil about 2 inches from source of heat. Broil 5 to 8 minutes, brushing occasionally with melted butter, until fish flakes easily when tested with a fork. Blend the parsley and dill into the softened butter and spread over the cooked fish. Serve immediately with lemon wedges.

YIELD: *6 servings.*

CODFISH BALLS

> ½ *pound boneless dried salted codfish*
> 3 *small boiling potatoes*
> 1 *tablespoon butter or margarine*
> 2 *eggs, beaten*
> ⅛ *teaspoon pepper*
> ¼ *cup chopped parsley*
> *Oil for deep-frying*
> *Parsley*
> *Tartar sauce*

Place codfish in a bowl and cover with boiling water. Let cool 1 hour; drain. Cut codfish in 1½-inch pieces and cover again with boiling water. Cool 1 hour and drain. Peel potatoes; put into saucepan. Place fish on top of potatoes. Add enough water barely to cover. Cover and boil gently until potatoes are tender, 15 to 20 minutes. Increase heat and shake pan gently from time to time to evaporate any remaining liquid. Mash thoroughly. Add next 4 ingredients, mix lightly but thoroughly. Cool; form into balls, using ¼ cup of mixture for each. Fry in oil heated to 350° F. about 5 minutes, until golden brown; turn occasionally. Drain on absorbent paper; garnish with parsley. Serve with tartar sauce.

YIELD: *8 codfish balls.*

NEW ENGLAND SALT CODFISH DINNER

1½ to 2 pounds boneless dried salted codfish
3 tablespoons butter or margarine
3 tablespoons flour
¾ teaspoon salt
⅛ teaspoon pepper
1 cup milk
½ cup light cream
2 hard-cooked eggs, diced
6 potatoes, cooked
12 small beets, cooked
6 small onions, cooked
Paprika

Place codfish in a bowl and cover with boiling water. Let cool 1 hour; drain. Cut into serving portions. Cover again with boiling water. Cool 1 hour and drain. Melt butter in saucepan; blend in flour, salt, and pepper. Gradually add milk and light cream and cook, stirring constantly, until mixture thickens and comes to a boil. Remove from heat; stir in eggs. Place fish on serving platter; top with sauce and surround with cooked vegetables. Sprinkle sauce with paprika.

YIELD: *6 servings.*

CREAMED CODFISH IN POTATO RING

½ pound boneless dried salted codfish
2 tablespoons butter or margarine
2 tablespoons flour
2 cups milk
4 hard-cooked eggs, sliced
4 cups well-seasoned mashed potatoes
Paprika or chopped parsley, optional

Place codfish in a bowl and cover with boiling water. Let cool 1 hour; drain. Flake codfish and cover again with boiling water. Cool 1 hour and drain. Melt butter in a saucepan; blend in flour. Gradually add milk and cook, stirring constantly, until mixture thickens and comes to a boil. Add flaked fish and eggs. Arrange the hot mashed potatoes around the edge of serving platter and pour the creamed fish in the center. If desired, sprinkle with paprika or chopped parsley.

YIELD: *6 servings.*

PERCH FILLETS

¼ cup butter or margarine
2 tablespoons chopped onion
½ teaspoon salt
⅛ teaspoon pepper
3 cups soft bread cubes
½ cup grated sharp cheese
¼ cup water
4 perch fillets

Melt butter in saucepan; add onion and cook until tender. Combine with salt, pepper, soft bread cubes, cheese, and water. Place ½ cup stuffing on skin side of each perch fillet. Roll up and place in a greased baking pan. Bake in a 400° F. oven 30 minutes.

YIELD: *4 servings.*

BAKED POLLOCK WITH OYSTER DRESSING

1 (3-pound) pollock, dressed
Salt
Pepper
1 pint oysters, chopped
½ cup cracker crumbs
½ cup milk
½ teaspoon salt
¼ teaspoon pepper
2 teaspoons melted butter
Lemon wedges

Sprinkle cavity of pollock with salt and pepper. Combine remaining ingredients except lemon. Stuff fish and fasten with picks. Place in oiled baking dish. Make 3 or 4 gashes in back of fish; fill gashes with additional bits of butter. Bake in a 400° F. oven 12 minutes per pound. Serve with lemon wedges.

YIELD: *6 servings.*

MACKEREL—SHEEPSCOT-BAY STYLE

1 large onion, finely chopped
1 large carrot, finely chopped
½ green pepper, finely chopped
¾ cup vinegar

½ *teaspoon salt*
1 *tablespoon chopped parsley*
¼ *teaspoon dried leaf thyme*
1 *bay leaf*
2 *mackerel, about 2 pounds each, dressed*

Place onion, carrot, green pepper, vinegar, salt, parsley, thyme, and bay leaf in a saucepan. Cook over low heat 20 minutes. Remove bay leaf. Place the mackerel in a greased baking dish, pour sauce over and around the mackerel. Bake in a 400° F. oven 25 to 30 minutes.

YIELD: *4 servings.*

BAKED STUFFED BLUEFISH

1 *(3-pound) bluefish, dressed*
Salt
Pepper
1½ *cups day-old bread crumbs*
2 *tablespoons chopped onion*
2 *tablespoons finely chopped celery*
¼ *teaspoon salt*
1 *teaspoon poultry seasoning*
2 *tablespoons melted butter or margarine*
¼ *cup water*
Lemon wedges

Sprinkle cavity of bluefish with salt and pepper. Combine remaining ingredients except lemon. Stuff fish and fasten with picks. Place in oiled baking dish. Make 3 or 4 gashes in back of fish; fill gashes with additional bits of butter. Bake in a 400° F. oven 12 minutes per pound. Serve with lemon wedges.

YIELD: *6 servings.*

FILLET OF FLOUNDER CORINTH

1 tablespoon butter or margarine
1 cup chopped parsley, divided
4 flounder fillets
1 teaspoon seafood seasoning
1 cup finely chopped onion
3 tablespoons olive oil, divided
3 large ripe tomatoes, divided
Dry white wine
2 tablespoons lemon juice
1 teaspoon dried dillweed
⅛ teaspoon garlic powder
¼ teaspoon pepper

Rub bottom and sides of a 9×12-inch glass baking dish with butter. Sprinkle ½ cup of the parsley in bottom of buttered dish. Place flounder on top. Sprinkle seafood seasoning over fish. Cook onions in 2 tablespoons of the oil until tender. Crush 1 ripe tomato in a sieve, catching all juice in a 1-cup measure. Discard pulp; add wine to tomato juice to make 1 cup liquid. Add to onion with lemon juice, dillweed, garlic powder, and pepper. Stir in remaining ½ cup chopped parsley. Spread over fish. Slice remaining tomatoes into thick slices. Arrange over top of onion mixture. Sprinkle with remaining tablespoon oil. Bake in 350° F. oven 25 to 30 minutes until sauce bubbles and fish flakes easily when tested with a fork.

YIELD: *4 servings.*

ROLLED STUFFED FISH FILLETS

2½ cups toasted bread cubes
½ teaspoon salt

¼ *cup chopped celery*
¼ *cup minced onion*
¼ *teaspoon pepper*
¼ *teaspoon dried leaf marjoram or sage*
1 *tablespoon melted butter or margarine*
⅓ *cup milk*
1 *teaspoon lemon juice*
6 *perch or flounder fillets*

Combine toasted bread cubes, salt, celery, onion, pepper, marjoram, butter, milk, and lemon juice. Place stuffing on each fillet, roll up jelly-roll fashion and tie with string. Place in a greased shallow pan. Bake in 375° F. oven 30 minutes.

YIELD: *6 servings.*

FILLET OF FLOUNDER MEDITERRANEAN

3 *tablespoons butter or margarine, divided*
4 *small flounder fillets*
1 *can (8 ounces) tomato sauce with mushrooms*
2 *tablespoons minced onion*
½ *teaspoon seafood seasoning*
1 *tablespoon parsley*
2 *tablespoons lemon juice*

Spread 1 tablespoon of butter on bottom and sides of a shallow baking dish. Arrange fillets in dish. Melt remaining 2 tablespoons of butter. Combine with tomato sauce, onion, seafood seasoning, parsley, and lemon juice. Spoon sauce over fish. Bake in 300° F. oven 25 minutes until fish is done.

YIELD: *4 servings.*

BAKED FLOUNDER FRANÇOISE

4 flounder fillets
2 tablespoons mustard sauce
1 cup soft bread crumbs
½ teaspoon fines herbes
⅛ teaspoon dried leaf marjoram
2 tablespoons melted butter
Tartar sauce

Brush flounder generously on both sides with mustard sauce and arrange in shallow well-greased baking pan. Toss bread crumbs with remaining ingredients; sprinkle over fish. Bake in 400° F. oven 20 to 25 minutes until fish flakes easily and crumbs are crisp and browned. Serve with tartar sauce.

YIELD: *4 servings.*

PORGY WITH TOMATO SAUCE

4 pounds porgies, dressed
3 tablespoons butter or margarine
3 tablespoons finely chopped onion
6 tablespoons chopped parsley, divided
2 cups water
1 can (6 ounces) tomato paste
½ teaspoon salt
¼ teaspoon pepper
½ bay leaf

Cut porgies in serving pieces. Melt butter in saucepan; add onion and 3 tablespoons parsley. Cook until onion is tender. Add water, tomato paste, and seasonings. Add porgies and place in shallow baking pan. Bake in 350° F. oven 30 to 35 minutes. Sprinkle with remaining chopped parsley.

YIELD: *4 to 6 servings.*

BAKED WHITEFISH

3 cups toasted bread cubes
1 cup chopped fresh tomatoes
½ cup chopped peeled cucumber
½ teaspoon salt
¼ teaspoon dried leaf marjoram
⅛ teaspoon pepper
2 tablespoons lemon juice
5 tablespoons melted butter or margarine, divided
1 (3-pound) whitefish, dressed

Combine toasted bread cubes, tomatoes, cucumbers, salt, marjoram, pepper, lemon juice, and 4 tablespoons butter. Line a large, shallow baking pan with foil. Grease foil. Place whitefish on greased foil and fill cavity with stuffing. Do not skewer. Brush fish with remaining butter. Bake in 350° F. oven 30 minutes.

YIELD: *6 servings.*

BROILED HADDOCK WITH SHRIMP SAUCE

¼ cup butter or margarine
2 tablespoons flour
½ teaspoon paprika
½ teaspoon salt
Dash cayenne
1½ cups water
¾ cup instant nonfat dry milk
½ teaspoon Worcestershire sauce
1 cup diced cooked shrimp
1 teaspoon lemon juice
1 tablespoon chopped parsley
1½ pounds haddock fillets
2 tablespoons melted butter
Pepper

Melt butter in a saucepan; blend in flour. Remove from heat and add paprika, salt, cayenne pepper, water, and nonfat dry milk. Cook, stirring constantly, until mixture thickens and comes to a boil. Remove from heat and add Worcestershire sauce, shrimp, lemon juice, and parsley. Keep sauce warm while broiling haddock. Place haddock on foil-covered broiler pan. Brush with melted butter; sprinkle lightly with salt and pepper. Broil 2 inches from heat 6 to 10 minutes or until fish flakes easily when tested with a fork. Place on serving platter; top with sauce.

YIELD: *4 to 6 servings.*

CIOPPINO

½ cup chopped green pepper
½ cup chopped onion
2 tablespoons chopped parsley
2 cloves garlic, minced
¼ cup olive oil
2 cans (10½ ounces each) condensed tomato soup
1 soup can water
¼ teaspoon dried leaf basil
1 bay leaf
¼ teaspoon grated lemon rind
⅛ teaspoon salt
Dash pepper
¼ cup dry white wine
1 pound haddock fillets, cut in 2-inch pieces
1 pound shrimp, shelled and deveined
½ pound cooked crab meat

Cook green pepper, onion, parsley, and garlic in olive oil until vegetables are tender. Stir in soup, water, basil, bay leaf, lemon rind, salt, and pepper. Cook over low heat about 10 minutes to blend flavors. Add remaining ingredients. Cook 10 minutes longer, stirring occasionally.

YIELD: *6 to 8 servings.*

HADDOCK FILLETS WITH OYSTER STUFFING AND SAUCE

½ cup chopped oysters
½ cup fine dry bread crumbs
2 tablespoons chopped celery
½ teaspoon salt
⅛ teaspoon pepper
2 tablespoons melted butter
2 haddock fillets
Lemon juice
2 slices salt pork
Lemon wedges

Combine oysters, crumbs, celery, seasonings, and butter. Place 1 fillet on a greased ovenproof platter, skin side down. Sprinkle with additional salt and pepper and lemon juice. Spread with stuffing. Over this place the other fillet. Sprinkle with salt and pepper. Place salt pork on top and bake in a 375° F. oven about 25 minutes. Serve with hot Oyster Sauce (below) and garnish with lemon wedges.

YIELD: *4 servings.*

OYSTER SAUCE

3 tablespoons butter or margarine
3 tablespoons flour
¼ teaspoon salt
⅛ teaspoon pepper
1 cup milk
12 chopped oysters
2 teaspoons lemon juice
1 tablespoon minced parsley

Melt butter in saucepan; blend in flour, salt, and pepper. Gradually add milk and cook, stirring constantly, until mixture

thickens and comes to a boil. Add oysters and lemon juice;
heat to serving temperature. Sprinkle with parsley before serving.

YIELD: *2 cups.*

FILLET OF HADDOCK SUBLIME

2 pounds haddock fillets
4 thick slices tomato
4 large mushrooms, sliced
1 teaspoon salt
2 teaspoons chopped chives
¾ cup dry white wine
¼ cup butter or margarine
1½ tablespoons flour
Dash cayenne
½ cup light cream

Fold fillets in half and place in buttered shallow baking dish.
Arrange tomatoes and mushrooms over fish. Sprinkle with salt
and chives and pour in wine. Cover baking dish with foil and
bake in a 400° F. oven 25 to 30 minutes. While fish bakes, melt
butter in saucepan; blend in flour and cayenne. Drain liquid
from fish into this mixture; add cream and cook, stirring constantly, until mixture thickens and comes to a boil. Pour sauce
over baked fillets and serve at once.

YIELD: *4 to 6 servings.*

FILLETS OF HADDOCK SHALLOT

4 haddock fillets
Salt
White pepper

2 tablespoons butter
2 teaspoons chopped shallots
⅓ cup white wine
1½ tablespoons butter
1½ tablespoons flour
⅓ cup milk
1½ cups green seedless grapes
Fresh lemon wedges

Sprinkle each fillet lightly with salt and pepper. Roll up and fasten with toothpicks. Melt 2 tablespoons butter in 10-inch skillet. Stir in shallots and wine. Add haddock. Cover and cook slowly 10 to 12 minutes. Turn fillets once. Remove fish to an ovenproof platter and keep warm while making the sauce. Cook liquid remaining in pan until reduced about one third. Blend butter and flour together. Add to liquid in pan. Stir in milk and cook about 2 minutes. Arrange grapes on platter around fish. Pour sauce over top. Brown quickly under broiler. Serve immediately, garnished with lemon wedges.

YIELD: *4 servings.*

FISH PARMESAN

3 tablespoons butter or margarine
3 tablespoons flour
½ teaspoon onion salt
1 teaspoon Worcestershire sauce
1¼ cups milk
1 can (8 ounces) peas, drained
1 package (12 ounces) frozen perch or pike fillets,
    thawed
½ cup grated Parmesan cheese
Paprika

Melt butter in a saucepan; blend in flour, salt, and Worcestershire sauce. Gradually add milk and cook, stirring constantly,

until mixture thickens and comes to a boil. Add peas. Divide
fish into 4 ramekins; top with sauce. Sprinkle each serving with
2 tablespoons Parmesan cheese; top with dash of paprika. Bake
in a 400° F. oven 15 to 20 minutes; brown under broiler 2 to 3
minutes before serving.

YIELD: 4 servings.

TWIN PIKE

6 tablespoons butter or margarine, divided
1 cup chopped celery
½ cup chopped onion
1 quart soft bread crumbs
2 tablespoons grated lemon rind
1 teaspoon salt
2 teaspoons paprika
¼ cup diced peeled lemon
½ cup sour cream
2 pike or trout, dressed

Melt 4 tablespoons butter in saucepan. Add celery and onion
and cook until tender. Combine with soft bread crumbs,
lemon rind, salt, paprika, diced lemon, and sour cream. Place
2½ cups stuffing in cavities of each fish. Do not skewer. Place
fish in a large greased baking pan and brush with remaining
butter. Bake in 400° F. oven 10 minutes. Lower heat to 350° F.
and bake 20 minutes longer.

YIELD: 6 servings.

CURRIED FISH

2 pounds cod or halibut
4 tablespoons butter or margarine
1 tablespoon chopped green pepper

1 small onion, chopped
¼ cup chopped celery
3 tablespoons flour
1 teaspoon curry powder
⅛ teaspoon Tabasco
Salt
3 cups hot cooked rice
2 tablespoons chopped parsley

Simmer the fish about 10 minutes in a small quantity of water in a covered skillet; then drain. If necessary, add water to fish liquid to make 2 cups; reserve. Melt butter in saucepan; add green pepper, onion, and celery; cook until tender. Blend in flour. Gradually add reserved fish liquid and cook, stirring constantly, until mixture thickens and comes to a boil. Stir in curry powder, Tabasco, and salt. Remove the skin and bones from the fish, arrange on a heated platter with a border of rice. Pour the hot sauce over the fish and sprinkle with parsley.

YIELD: *6 servings.*

HALIBUT STEAK

3 tablespoons melted butter or margarine, divided
3 cups soft bread cubes
¼ cup chopped celery
¼ cup chopped dill pickle
1 tablespoon lemon juice
2 tablespoons hot water
½ teaspoon salt
½ teaspoon dried leaf basil
½ teaspoon crumbled dry dill or dill seeds
⅛ teaspoon pepper
2 halibut steaks

Combine 2 tablespoons butter, bread cubes, celery, dill pickle, lemon juice, water, salt, basil, dill, and pepper. Place 1 fish steak in a greased baking dish. Place stuffing on fish and cover with the other fish steak. Fasten together with toothpicks. Brush top with remaining butter. Bake in 350° F. oven 45 minutes.

YIELD: *4 servings.*

HERBED FISH BAKE

> *2 pounds halibut steak*
> *1 can (4 ounces) sliced mushrooms*
> *2 tablespoons flour*
> *1 teaspoon salt*
> *½ teaspoon dried leaf tarragon*
> *⅛ teaspoon pepper*
> *1½ cups sour cream*
> *Paprika*
> *Lemon slices*
> *¼ cup chopped parsley*

Butter a large shallow casserole; add halibut. Drain mushrooms reserving 3 tablespoons mushroom liquid. Combine mushrooms with liquid, flour, salt, tarragon, and pepper. Gently fold in sour cream. Spoon mixture over halibut; sprinkle with paprika. Bake in 350° F. oven 30 minutes. Remove from oven; dip lemon slices in parsley and arrange on halibut. Serve with additional lemon slices, if desired.

YIELD: *4 servings.*

HALIBUT STUFFED WITH CRAB MEAT

> *5 tablespoons butter or margarine, divided*
> *1 tablespoon minced onion*
> *1 tablespoon minced celery*
> *1 tablespoon minced parsley*

½ *cup cracker crumbs*
1 can (7¾ ounces) crab meat
1 egg
½ teaspoon salt
⅛ teaspoon pepper
4 halibut steaks

Melt 2 tablespoons butter in small skillet; add onion, celery, and parsley and cook 5 minutes. Remove from heat; add cracker crumbs, crab meat, egg, salt, and pepper. Mix thoroughly. Cut the halibut steaks into halves; spread half the steaks with stuffing, cover with remaining halibut. Brush with 3 tablespoons melted butter. Place in a shallow pan; bake in a 350° F. oven 30 to 40 minutes, brushing frequently with melted butter.

YIELD: *4 servings.*

BAKED HALIBUT WITH TART BUTTER SAUCE

½ cup butter
1 egg yolk
1½ teaspoons lemon juice
¼ teaspoon dry mustard
Dash cayenne
¼ cup toasted sliced almonds
1 tablespoon chopped parsley
2 to 3 pounds halibut steak, 1 inch thick

Melt butter in saucepan; cool slightly. Blend together egg yolk, lemon juice, mustard, and cayenne. Slowly add butter, beating constantly, until thick. Stir in almonds and parsley. Place halibut in a buttered 13×9-inch baking pan. Spread with butter mixture. Bake in a 375° F. oven 20 to 30 minutes or until fish flakes easily with a fork.

YIELD: *6 to 8 servings.*

STUFFED HALIBUT STEAK

1 dozen oysters
1 cup cracker crumbs
½ teaspoon salt
⅛ teaspoon pepper
1 tablespoon chopped parsley
2 tablespoons melted butter or margarine
2 halibut steaks
1 tablespoon lemon juice
Melted butter for basting
Lemon slices

Chop oysters. Add crumbs, salt, pepper, parsley, and butter
and mix well. Place 1 halibut steak on greased shallow baking
dish; sprinkle with lemon juice and additional salt and pepper.
Spread with oyster stuffing and place second slice of halibut
on top. Fasten together with small skewers; brush with melted
butter. Bake in a 350° F. oven about 30 to 40 minutes, brushing frequently with melted butter. Serve with slices of lemon.

YIELD: *4 to 6 servings.*

HALIBUT LOAF WITH LOBSTER SAUCE

2 cups light cream
2½ cups soft bread crumbs
1 tablespoon butter or margarine
1 teaspoon salt
¼ teaspoon celery salt
⅛ teaspoon pepper
1 pound chopped raw halibut
4 egg whites

Scald cream in saucepan; add bread crumbs, butter, salt, celery
salt, and pepper. Add chopped halibut and mix well. Cook
gently until thoroughly heated. Fold in the stiffly beaten
egg whites. Place in a greased casserole and set in pan of hot

water. Bake in a 350° F. oven 1 hour. Serve with Lobster Sauce (below).

YIELD: *8 servings.*

LOBSTER SAUCE

3 tablespoons butter or margarine
3 tablespoons flour
1 teaspoon salt
⅛ teaspoon pepper
1 cup milk
½ cup heavy cream
1½ cups cut-up cooked lobster

Melt butter in saucepan; blend in flour and seasonings. Gradually add milk and cream and cook, stirring constantly, until mixture thickens and comes to a boil. Add lobster; heat to serving temperature.

YIELD: *3¼ cups.*

HALIBUT SALAD MOLD

1½ tablespoons flour
½ teaspoon salt
2 teaspoons mustard
2 teaspoons sugar
1 egg, slightly beaten
½ cup evaporated milk
5 tablespoons lemon juice
1 envelope unflavored gelatin
¼ cup cold water
¼ teaspoon celery salt
1 cup flaked, cooked halibut
½ cup heavy cream, whipped
Lettuce
Olives
Pimiento strips

Put the flour, salt, mustard, and sugar in top of double boiler.
Add egg, evaporated milk, and lemon juice. Stir over hot water
until mixture thickens. Sprinkle gelatin on cold water to
soften. Add to hot mixture with celery salt. Stir until gelatin is
dissolved. Add the flaked halibut. Cool, add cream. Turn into
a 1-quart mold or fish-shaped mold and chill. Unmold on crisp
lettuce and garnish with olives and strips of pimiento.

YIELD: *4 servings.*

NEW ENGLAND CRAB MEAT SAUCE

¼ cup butter or margarine
2 tablespoons minced onion
¼ cup flour
1 teaspoon salt
Few grains cayenne
1 can (6 ounces) mushrooms
1½ cups sour cream
1 can (7½ ounces) crab meat
2 egg yolks
1 tablespoon dry sherry
1 tablespoon chopped parsley

Melt butter in saucepan; add onion and cook until tender.
Blend in flour, salt, and pepper. Drain mushrooms. Add enough
water to mushroom liquid to make ¾ cup. Add to saucepan
and cook, stirring constantly, until mixture thickens and comes
to a boil. Stir in sour cream, crab meat, egg yolks, sherry,
mushrooms and parsley. Continue cooking over low heat until
thickened. Serve on Yankee Noodle Dandy (below).

YIELD: *4 servings.*

YANKEE NOODLE DANDY

1 cup fresh bread cubes
2 tablespoons butter or margarine
2 cups egg noodles
1 cup shredded Cheddar cheese

Brown bread cubes in butter or margarine. Cook noodles according to directions on package. Drain. Mix noodles, cheese, and bread cubes.

YIELD: *3 servings.*

CRAB-CORN STEW

2 tablespoons butter or margarine
¼ cup chopped onion
2 cans (7¾ ounces each) crab meat
1 can (8 ounces) whole-kernel corn, drained
2 teaspoons Worcestershire sauce
1 pint heavy cream
Salt
Pepper
Paprika

Melt butter in a large saucepan; add onion and cook until tender. Add crab meat; heat 5 minutes. Add remaining ingredients except paprika; heat to serving temperature. Sprinkle with paprika.

YIELD: *6 servings.*

ASPARAGUS-TOPPED CRAB IMPERIAL

1 package (10 ounces) frozen asparagus, cooked
¼ cup butter or margarine
2 tablespoons chopped green pepper
1 tablespoon chopped onion
¼ cup flour
1¼ teaspoons salt
½ teaspoon Ac'cent
⅔ cup instant nonfat dry milk
1¾ cups water
2 egg yolks
2 packages (6 ounces each) frozen crab meat, thawed
1 teaspoon Worcestershire sauce
1 teaspoon dried leaf tarragon
1 tablespoon lemon juice
½ cup grated Parmesan cheese

Place asparagus in a 1½-quart baking dish. Melt butter in a saucepan; add green pepper and onion and cook until tender. Blend in flour, salt, and Ac'cent. Mix nonfat dry milk and water; add to flour mixture. Cook, stirring constantly, until mixture thickens and comes to a boil. Beat egg yolks until light and lemon-colored. Mix a small amount of sauce with yolks; return to saucepan. Stir until smooth. Add crab meat, Worcestershire sauce, tarragon, and lemon juice. Pour over asparagus. Sprinkle with Parmesan cheese and bake in 400° F. oven 20 minutes.

YIELD: *4 to 6 servings.*

CRAB MEAT CASSEROLE

6 tablespoons butter or margarine, divided
2 tablespoons finely chopped onion

½ cup finely chopped celery
3 tablespoons flour
¾ teaspoon salt
2 cups half and half
¼ cup dry sherry
1 egg, beaten
¼ teaspoon Tabasco
3 cups cooked crab meat
2 tablespoons chopped parsley
1½ cups fine fresh bread cubes
Lemon twists, optional
Parsley sprigs, optional

Heat 4 tablespoons butter in saucepan. Add onion and celery and cook until onion is tender. Blend in flour and salt. Gradually add half and half and sherry. Cook, stirring constantly, until mixture thickens and comes to a boil. Remove from heat; gradually add small amount of sauce to egg, stirring rapidly. Return egg mixture to sauce; add Tabasco and mix well. Add crab meat and parsley. Turn into 6 individual shells or casseroles. Melt remaining 2 tablespoons butter; add bread cubes and toss. Sprinkle over crab mixture. Bake in 350° F. oven 20 minutes. If desired, garnish each serving with a lemon twist and a sprig of parsley.

Yield: *6 servings.*

DEVILED CRAB

1 can (10½ ounces) condensed cream of celery soup
1 can (7¾ ounces) crab meat
2 tablespoons chopped green pepper
1 tablespoon chopped onion
2 teaspoons lemon juice
1 teaspoon Worcestershire sauce
½ teaspoon prepared mustard
4 tablespoons buttered bread crumbs

Combine all ingredients except bread crumbs; spoon into 4 small buttered baking dishes. Sprinkle crumbs over top. Bake in a 350° F. oven 30 minutes.

YIELD: *4 servings.*

CRAB MEAT-VEGETABLE CLUB SALAD

> *1 can (7¾ ounces) crab meat*
> *1 cup cottage cheese*
> *1 tablespoon finely chopped onion*
> *1 teaspon lemon juice*
> *½ teaspoon salt*
> *2 cups cooked green beans, chilled*
> *2 cups sliced cooked carrots, chilled*
> *Salad greens*
> *6 tomato wedges*
> *Radish slices*

Combine crab meat, cottage cheese, onion, lemon juice, and salt; mix well. For each serving, arrange crab-cheese mixture, green beans, and carrot slices on salad greens. Garnish with tomato wedges and radish slices.

YIELD: *4 to 6 servings.*

SALMON CROQUETTES

> *1 can (1 pound) salmon*
> *1 can (10¾ ounces) condensed cream of mushroom soup*
> *2 tablespoons lemon juice*
> *1 medium onion, finely chopped*
> *⅛ teaspoon Tabasco*
> *1 cup coarse cracker crumbs (about 18 salted soda*
> *crackers, coarsely rolled)*

¼ *cup milk*
1 *egg, beaten*
¾ *cup fine cracker crumbs*

Drain and flake salmon, and save salmon liquid for use in a sauce. Measure out 1 cup of the mushroom soup and add it to the flaked salmon. Stir in lemon juice, onion, Tabasco, and coarse cracker crumbs. Combine ingredients thoroughly and shape into 8 or 10 croquettes of desired form. Chill. When ready to cook, add milk to beaten egg. Roll each croquette in the fine cracker crumbs, then in the egg mixture, and again the cracker crumbs. Fry in hot deep fat (375° F.) for 3 to 5 minutes or until golden brown. Drain on absorbent paper. Combine remaining condensed cream of mushroom soup with canned salmon liquid; heat. Serve with croquettes.

YIELD: *4 or 5 servings.*

SALMON STOCKHOLM

½ *cup dry white wine*
½ *cup water*
¼ *teaspoon dried dillweed*
½ *teaspoon dried leaf thyme*
½ *teaspoon mustard seed, crushed*
1 *lemon, thinly sliced*
2 *tablespoons butter or margarine*
4 *salmon steaks*
2 *teaspoons cornstarch*
2 *tablespoons water*

Combine wine, water, dillweed, leaf thyme, mustard seed, lemon, and butter in a skillet; heat just to boiling. Add salmon steaks, cover, and simmer gently 15 minutes, or until fish flakes with fork. Remove fish to heated serving platter. Blend cornstarch and water. Blend into pan juices, stirring constantly, until mixture thickens and clears. Spoon over fish.

YIELD: *4 servings.*

SALMON STEAK

3 tablespoons butter or margarine, divided
¼ cup chopped celery
1 cup soft bread crumbs
1 tablespoon chopped parsley
½ cup chopped hard-cooked eggs
⅛ teaspoon salt
⅛ teaspoon paprika
6 salmon steaks, ½ inch thick
1 tablespoon grated Parmesan cheese

Melt 1 tablespoon butter in saucepan; add celery and cook until tender. Combine with soft bread crumbs, parsley, eggs, salt, and paprika. Arrange salmon steaks in a greased baking pan. Place ¼ cup stuffing in each of the openings formed by the ends of the fish. Sprinkle ½ teaspoon Parmesan cheese over the stuffing in each steak. Brush steaks with remaining butter. Bake in a 350° F. oven 25 to 30 minutes.

YIELD: *6 servings.*

SALMONBURGERS

1 can (1 pound) salmon, drained and flaked
1 cup soft bread crumbs
1 egg, beaten
½ teaspoon salt
⅛ teaspoon pepper
2 tablespoons finely chopped onion

8 hamburger buns, split, toasted
Butter
8 slices tomato

Combine salmon, bread crumbs, beaten egg, salt, pepper, and onion; mix thoroughly. Shape into 8 patties of about equal size. Heat the hamburger buns. Pan-fry patties in a little butter until browned on both sides. Place a patty in each bun; top with a slice of tomato.

YIELD: 8 salmonburgers.

SALMON CASSEROLES BOURGEOISE

2 tablespoons butter or margarine
1 tablespoon grated onion
1 cup sliced mushrooms
1 tablespoon flour
1 cup chicken broth
1 cup light cream
3 egg yolks, beaten
2 tablespoons dry white wine
1 can (8 ounces) salmon, drained and flaked
Paprika

Melt butter in saucepan; add onion and mushrooms and cook until tender. Blend in flour. Gradually add chicken broth and cream and cook, stirring constantly, until mixture thickens and comes to a boil. Add a small amount to the egg yolks, stirring rapidly. Return to saucepan and cook until thickened, about 2 minutes. Stir in wine and salmon. Turn into 4 individual casseroles. Sprinkle with paprika. Bake in a 350° F. oven 20 to 25 minutes.

YIELD: 4 servings.

SALMON SHORTCAKE

1 cup packaged biscuit mix
2 cups sour cream, divided
2 tablespoons grated American cheese
2 tablespoons butter
1 medium green pepper, finely chopped
3 tablespoons finely chopped onion
½ teaspoon salt
⅛ teaspoon pepper
1 tablespoon flour
1 can (10¾ ounces) condensed cream of mushroom
    soup
1 can (1 pound) salmon, drained and flaked

Combine biscuit mix and ½ cup of the sour cream. On greased baking sheet, drop 6 spoonfuls of batter; top each with 1 teaspoon of cheese. Bake in a 425° F. oven 12 to 15 minutes or until biscuits are a golden brown. Keep biscuits hot. Melt butter in a saucepan; add green pepper and onion and cook until tender. Blend in salt, pepper, and flour. Stir in soup, remaining sour cream, and salmon. Cook over low heat, stirring constantly, until mixture begins to bubble. To serve, split biscuits in half. Spoon salmon mixture over each bottom half; cover with biscuit top.

YIELD: 6 servings.

SALMON PATTIES

1 can (1 pound) salmon
1 cup saltine cracker crumbs
1 tablespoon minced onion

1 egg white
⅔ cup evaporated milk
⅓ cup finely chopped celery
1 tablespoon lemon juice
3 tablespoons butter

Drain salmon, reserving liquid. Flake salmon in its liquid in a mixing bowl. Mix in cracker crumbs, onion, egg white, evaporated milk, celery, and lemon juice. Let stand 5 minutes to let crumbs absorb moisture. Divide into 8 equal portions and shape into patties. Melt butter in a large skillet. Add the patties and cook over low heat until golden brown, about 5 minutes on each side, turning just once. Serve with Dill Sauce (below).

YIELD: *4 servings.*

DILL SAUCE

2 tablespoons butter or margarine
2 tablespoons flour
1 cup evaporated milk
⅓ cup water
1 egg yolk, beaten
¼ teaspoon salt
Dash pepper
1 teaspoon dried dillweed

Melt butter in a saucepan; blend in flour. Gradually add evaporated milk and water. Cook over low heat, stirring constantly, until mixture thickens and comes to a boil. Stir a little of the hot sauce into the beaten egg yolk. Pour this mixture into the remaining hot sauce and continue cooking and stirring until mixture comes to a boil once more. Season with salt, pepper, and dillweed.

DILLY SALMON PIE

½ cup shredded process American cheese
1 tablespoon flour
1 (9-inch) unbaked pastry shell
1 can (1 pound) salmon, drained and flaked
1 cup drained canned peas
3 eggs
1 cup evaporated milk
1 tablespoon minced onion
⅛ teaspoon pepper
1 teaspoon dried dillweed
½ cup cheese cracker crumbs, optional

Combine cheese and flour. Spread half of cheese-flour evenly in bottom of pastry shell. Top with half of the salmon, then half of the peas. Repeat layers of salmon and peas. Top with remaining cheese. Beat eggs in a mixing bowl; blend in evaporated milk, onion, pepper, and dillweed. Pour carefully over ingredients in pie shell. Top with cheese crackers, if desired. Bake in 425° F. oven 15 minutes. Reduce heat to 325° F., cover lightly with aluminum foil, and bake an additional 30 minutes or until knife inserted in center comes out clean.

YIELD: 6 servings.

SALMON SCALLOP SUPREME

2 cups coarsely crushed salted cracker crumbs
⅓ cup melted butter or margarine
1 tablespoon minced parsley
1 teaspoon grated onion
Dash pepper

1 can (1 pound) salmon, drained and coarsely flaked
1 cup light cream

Combine cracker crumbs, butter, parsley, onion, and pepper.
Spread 1 cup crumb mixture in 9-inch pie pan. Cover with
salmon; sprinkle remaining crumbs over salmon. Pour cream
over crumbs. Bake in a 400° F. oven 20 minutes, or until
crumbs are toasted and casserole is thoroughly heated.

YIELD: *4 servings.*

SALMON CRÊPES BAYOU

1 can (1 pound) salmon
Milk
1 teaspoon chopped onion
3 tablespoons butter or margarine
¼ cup flour
¼ teaspoon salt
⅛ teaspoon white pepper
⅛ teaspoon nutmeg
2 egg yolks, beaten
2 tablespoons grated Parmesan cheese
2 tablespoons dry sherry
12 Crêpes (below)
2 slices lemon, cut into sixths
Parsley

Drain salmon; reserve liquid. Add enough milk to liquid to
make 1½ cups; reserve. Cook onion in butter until tender.
Blend in flour and seasonings. Gradually add salmon-milk mixture and cook, stirring constantly, until mixture thickens and
comes to a boil. Stir a little of the hot sauce into egg yolks; add
to remaining sauce, stirring constantly. Add cheese and sherry
and stir until blended. Mix ½ cup of the sauce with the

salmon. Blend well. Reserve remaining sauce to serve with crêpes. Spread about 2 tablespoons of salmon mixture on each crêpe. Roll like a jelly roll. Place crêpes on a greased cookie sheet. Heat in a 350° F. oven 10 to 15 minutes. Heat the sauce. Arrange the crêpes in a circle in a chafing dish. Garnish each crêpe with lemon and parsley. Place sauce in the center.

YIELD: *6 servings.*

CRÊPES

¾ cup sifted all-purpose flour
¼ teaspoon salt
2 eggs, beaten
1 cup milk

Sift dry ingredients together. Combine eggs and milk. Add gradually to flour and salt; stir only until batter is smooth. Drop 2 tablespoons of batter onto a hot greased griddle or frying pan. Fry about 2 minutes or until crêpe is browned on the underside; turn, and fry until the bottom is browned.

YIELD: *12 crêpes.*

CREAMED SALMON

1 tablespoon butter or margarine
¼ cup chopped onion
1 can (10¾ ounces) condensed cream of mushroom
     soup
⅓ to ½ cup milk
1 can (8 ounces) salmon, drained and flaked
¾ cup cooked green beans
1 tablespoon lemon juice

Melt butter in saucepan; add onion and cook until tender.
Blend in soup, milk, salmon, green beans, and lemon juice.
Heat to serving temperature. Serve over toast or rice.

YIELD: *3 to 4 servings.*

SALMON CHEESE CASSEROLE

4 tablespoons butter or margarine
¼ cup flour
1 cup milk
1½ cups cottage cheese
2 eggs
1½ teaspoons Worcestershire sauce
½ teaspoon salt
½ teaspoon paprika
1 tablespoon lemon juice
1 can (1 pound) salmon, drained and flaked
1 cup cooked lima beans
¼ cup chopped ripe olives
4 tablespoons grated Parmesan cheese

Melt butter in saucepan. Blend in flour. Gradually add milk
and cook, stirring constantly, until mixture thickens and comes
to a boil. Cover and remove from heat. Beat cottage cheese
with rotary beater until almost smooth; add eggs and continue
beating until well blended. Stir in Worcestershire, salt, and
paprika. Gradually add lemon juice. Add slightly cooled white
sauce. Gently fold in salmon, lima beans, and olives. Turn into
a 1½-quart casserole; sprinkle with cheese. Bake in a 325° F.
oven 40 minutes.

YIELD: *4 servings.*

SALMON RICE SOUFFLÉ

⅓ cup precooked rice
⅓ cup water
2 tablespoons butter or margarine
½ teaspoon salt
1 can (8 ounces) salmon, drained and flaked
½ cup crushed potato chips
⅓ cup milk
1½ cups shredded Cheddar cheese
7 egg yolks
7 egg whites

Preheat oven to 350° F. Set a greased 2-quart loaf pan in a shallow baking pan; place in oven. Pour boiling water around loaf pan to depth of at least 1 inch; let loaf pan heat while preparing soufflé. Combine rice, water, butter, and salt and cook according to package directions. Combine cooked rice, salmon, potato chips, milk, and cheese. Beat egg yolks until thick and lemon-colored; fold into salmon mixture. Beat egg whites until stiff, but not dry. Fold beaten whites gently into salmon mixture. Pour into hot loaf pan. Bake until puffy, delicately browned, and a silver knife inserted halfway between center and outside edge comes out clean, about 1 hour. Serve immediately.

YIELD: *4 to 6 servings.*

SALMON CURRY

1 can (1 pound) salmon
¼ cup chopped onion
3 tablespoons butter or margarine

> 3 tablespoons flour
> 1½ teaspoons curry powder
> ½ teaspoon salt
> ¼ teaspoon ginger
> Dash pepper
> 2 cups salmon liquid with milk
> 3 cups cooked rice

Drain salmon, reserving liquid. Break salmon into large pieces. Cook onion in butter in saucepan until tender. Blend in flour and seasonings. Gradually add salmon-milk mixture and cook, stirring constantly, until mixture thickens and comes to a boil. Add salmon; heat. Serve over rice with any of the following curry condiments.

YIELD: *6 servings.*

Curry Condiments: Chopped hard-cooked egg, shredded toasted coconut, chopped nuts, chopped green pepper, chopped tomatoes, chopped onion, or crystallized ginger.

SALMON LOAF WITH CURRY SAUCE

> 1 can (1 pound) salmon, drained and flaked
> 1 cup milk
> 1 cup fine dry bread crumbs
> 1 egg, slightly beaten
> 2 tablespoons chopped parsley
> 2 tablespoons chopped onion
> 2 teaspoons lemon juice
> ¼ teaspoon salt
> Dash pepper

Combine all ingredients; pack into greased 9×5×3-inch loaf pan. Bake in 375° F. oven 25 minutes or until loaf is firm in center. Remove from oven; let stand 5 minutes in pan; turn out onto heated serving platter. Cook 1 tablespoon chopped onion in 1 tablespoon butter or margarine until tender. Blend in 1 can (10½ ounces) condensed cream of celery or mushroom soup and ¼ to ½ teaspoon curry powder; heat thoroughly. Serve with salmon loaf.

YIELD: *4 servings.*

SAVORY SALMON LOAF

1 can (1 pound) salmon, drained and flaked
1½ cups packaged poultry stuffing
¼ cup finely chopped celery
2 tablespoons minced onion
2 eggs, slightly beaten
1 can (10¾ ounces) condensed cream of mushroom
     soup

Combine all ingredients; pack into greased 9×5×3-inch loaf pan. Bake in 350° F. oven 45 to 50 minutes or until center is firm. Remove from oven; let stand 5 minutes in pan; turn out onto heated serving platter. Serve with tomato or cheese sauce.

YIELD: *4 to 6 servings.*

SALMON ROLL

3 tablespoons butter or margarine
¼ cup chopped onion
¼ cup chopped green pepper
3 tablespoons flour
1 teaspoon salt

¼ *teaspoon pepper*
2 *cups milk*
1 *can (1 pound) salmon, drained and flaked*
1 *cup drained cooked peas*
Paprika

Melt butter in saucepan; add onion and green pepper and cook until tender. Blend in flour, salt, and pepper. Gradually add milk and cook, stirring constantly, until mixture thickens and comes to a boil. Remove from heat and reserve. Prepare Biscuit Dough (below). Roll out to a 14×9-inch rectangle. Mix ¾ cup sauce with salmon. Spread evenly on biscuit dough. Roll from the long side as for jelly roll. Place seam down on a greased baking sheet. Bake in a 400° F. oven 35 minutes. Reheat remaining sauce with peas, spoon over slices of Salmon Roll, and sprinkle with paprika.

YIELD: *6 servings.*

BISCUIT DOUGH

2 *cups sifted all-purpose flour*
3 *teaspoons baking powder*
1 *teaspoon salt*
⅔ *cup salad oil*
⅔ *cup milk*

Sift together flour, baking powder, and salt. Stir in salad oil and milk. Mix well and form into a ball.

SALMON À LAZARE

1 tablespoon butter or margarine
½ cup sliced celery
2 tablespoons chopped onion
1 can (10¾ ounces) condensed cream of mushroom
*   soup*
½ cup milk
1 can (8 ounces) salmon, drained and flaked
2 tablespoons chopped pimiento
4 slices toast
Chopped parsley

Melt butter in saucepan; add celery and onion and cook until tender. Blend in soup; gradually stir in milk. Add salmon and pimiento. Heat to serving temperature. Serve over toast. Garnish with parsley.

YIELD: *4 servings.*

PINEAPPLE-GLAZED SALMON PATTIES

2 cans (8 ounces each) salmon, drained and flaked
¼ cup fine dry bread crumbs
2 tablespoons finely chopped onion
1 egg, beaten
⅓ cup evaporated milk
⅛ teaspoon pepper
⅛ teaspoon dried leaf thyme
¼ cup firmly packed brown sugar
2 teaspoons vinegar
¼ teaspoon dry mustard
1 teaspoon cornstarch

1 *teaspoon water*
½ *cup drained crushed pineapple*

Combine salmon, bread crumbs, onion, egg, milk, pepper, and thyme; mix well. Turn mixture into 6 lightly greased 3-inch muffin cups, filling about two thirds full. Round top with spoon. Bake in a 350° F. oven 10 minutes. Meanwhile, combine brown sugar, vinegar, and mustard. Heat to boiling point over medium heat and boil 1 minute, stirring occasionally. Blend cornstarch and water. Add cornstarch mixture and pineapple to saucepan and cook, stirring constantly, until thickened, about 3 minutes. Spoon pineapple glaze over patties. Bake 10 minutes. Remove from muffin pans with a spoon and serve.

YIELD: *6 servings.*

SALMON CASSOULET

1 *can (1 pound) salmon*
1 *cup uncooked elbow macaroni*
1 *tablespoon chopped green pepper*
1 *small clove garlic, finely chopped*
⅓ *cup butter or margarine*
⅓ *cup flour*
2 *teaspoons dried mustard*
¼ *teaspoon pepper*
2 *cups salmon liquid and milk*
1 *cup grated American cheese*
1 *cup cooked lima beans*

Drain salmon, reserving liquid. Flake salmon. Cook macaroni as directed on the package. Drain. Cook green pepper and garlic in butter in saucepan until tender. Blend in flour and seasonings. Gradually add salmon-milk mixture and cook, stirring constantly, until mixture thickens and comes to a boil.

Add cheese and continue cooking until cheese melts, stirring constantly. Arrange half of the macaroni, lima beans, salmon, and sauce in layers in a well-greased, 2-quart casserole. Repeat layers. Bake in 350° F. oven 25 to 30 minutes.

YIELD: *6 servings.*

SALMON FLORENTINE

1 can (1 pound) salmon
1 cup cooked drained spinach
4 tablespoons melted butter or margarine, divided
¼ teaspoon pepper
Dash nutmeg
2 tablespoons chopped onion
1 clove garlic, finely chopped
3 tablespoons flour
¼ teaspoon salt
1¼ cups salmon liquid and milk
2 tablespoons dry sherry
¼ cup grated Parmesan cheese
3 hard-cooked eggs, sliced
Watercress

Drain salmon, reserving liquid. Mash salmon. Chop spinach. Season with 2 tablespoons butter, pepper, and nutmeg. Spread seasoned spinach in a greased 8-inch round baking dish. Cook onion and garlic in 2 tablespoons butter in saucepan until tender. Blend in flour and salt. Gradually add salmon-milk mixture and cook, stirring constantly, until mixture thickens and comes to a boil. Add sherry and salmon. Blend thoroughly. Spoon over spinach; sprinkle with cheese. Bake in 350° F. oven 25 minutes. Garnish with egg slices and watercress.

YIELD: *6 servings.*

SPEEDY SALMON BAKE

1 can (8 ounces) salmon, drained and flaked
2 cans (about 1 pound each) spaghetti in tomato
sauce with cheese
1 tablespoon grated onion
½ teaspoon grated lemon rind
¼ teaspoon salt
⅛ teaspoon pepper
¼ cup grated Parmesan or shredded Cheddar cheese

Combine all ingredients except cheese; turn into greased 1½-quart baking dish. Sprinkle cheese over top. Bake in 375° F. oven 30 minutes.

YIELD: *4 servings.*

SALMON-ALMOND CASSEROLE

1 can (8 ounces) salmon, drained; reserve liquid
1 cup cooked rice
2 tablespoons butter or margarine
½ cup chopped onion
½ cup chopped green pepper
1 can (10¾ ounces) condensed cream of mushroom
soup
Milk
1¾ cups coarsely crushed potato chips
¼ cup blanched almonds

Drain and flake salmon, and save salmon liquid. Combine salmon with rice. Melt butter in saucepan; add onion and green pepper and cook until tender. Add to salmon mixture; mix gently. Blend soup, salmon liquid, and milk to make ⅔ cup. Place half the potato chips in a greased 1½-quart casserole. Cover with alternate layers of salmon mixture and soup mixture. Top with remaining potato chips. Sprinkle with blanched almonds. Bake uncovered in a 375° F. oven 30 minutes.

YIELD: *4 to 6 servings.*

SALMON PICKUPS

1 can (8 ounces) salmon, drained, flaked
1 package (3 ounces) cream cheese, softened
2 tablespoons sour cream
2 tablespoons chopped green olives
1 tablespoon grated onion
¼ teaspoon salt
Dash pepper
Minced parsley or chives, optional

Combine all ingredients except parsley; chill. Shape into half-inch balls. Roll in minced parsley or chives, if desired; chill. Serve on toothpicks.

YIELD: *36 salmon pickups.*

QUICK AND EASY SALMON CASSEROLE

1 can (8 ounces) salmon, drained, flaked; reserve
    liquid
Milk
1 can (10¾ ounces) condensed cream of
  mushroom soup

1½ cups cooked peas
1 cup unbroken potato chips

Combine salmon liquid and milk to make ¼ cup. Combine with soup, peas, and salmon in a greased 1-quart casserole. Top with potato chips. Bake in 375° F. oven 30 minutes.

YIELD: 4 servings.

BAKED SALMON INDIA

3 tablespoons butter or margarine
½ cup thinly sliced onion
½ cup chopped celery
1 cup very thinly sliced carrots
½ teaspoon curry powder
1 can (1 pound) salmon, drained, flaked; reserve
      liquid
1½ cups cooked rice
Milk
½ teaspoon salt
⅛ teaspoon pepper

Melt butter in saucepan. Add onion, celery, and carrots and cook over low heat until tender. Stir in curry powder. Combine salmon, vegetables, rice, salmon liquid, plus milk to make ½ cup, salt, and pepper. When thoroughly mixed turn into a greased 1½-quart casserole. Cover and bake in a 350° F. oven 30 minutes.

YIELD: 6 servings.

SALMON LOAF

1 can (1 pound) salmon
½ teaspoon salt
⅛ teaspoon pepper
¼ cup chopped celery
1 tablespoon minced onion
2 eggs, well beaten
½ cup fine cracker crumbs

Flake salmon and mix with salmon liquid. Combine with remaining ingredients. Mix well and pack into a small, greased loaf pan. Bake in 350° F. oven 45 minutes or until firm and lightly browned. Unmold on heated platter.

YIELD: *4 servings.*

SALMON À LA KING

1 can (1 pound) salmon, flaked; drain and reserve
liquid
¼ cup butter or margarine
½ cup chopped celery
½ cup chopped green pepper
¼ cup flour
½ teaspoon salt
1½ cups liquid (liquid from canned salmon plus milk
to make volume)
1 can (8 ounces) sliced mushrooms, drained
2 tablespoons chopped pimiento

Drain salmon and save liquid. Break salmon into bite-sized chunks. Melt butter in saucepan. Add celery and green pepper and cook over low heat until vegetables are tender. Blend in

flour and salt. Gradually add salmon liquid plus milk to make
1½ cups and cook, stirring constantly, until mixture thickens
and comes to a boil. Add salmon, mushrooms, and pimiento.
Heat thoroughly. Serve in patty shells, toast cups, or on cooked
rice.

YIELD: *6 servings.*

SALMON PIE

>*1 can (1 pound) salmon, flaked; drain and reserve liquid*
>*Milk*
>*½ cup soft bread crumbs*
>*1 teaspoon grated onion*
>*¼ teaspoon salt*
>*1 tablespoon chopped parsley*
>*1 teaspoon lemon juice*
>*½ teaspoon garlic salt*
>*2 eggs, slightly beaten*

Combine salmon liquid plus milk to make 1 cup. Combine
salmon and liquid. Stir in remaining ingredients. Turn into a
greased 8-inch pie pan and bake in 350° F. oven 45 minutes.

YIELD: *6 servings.*

SALMON BOATS

>*1 can (8 ounces) salmon, drained and flaked*
>*1 cup sliced celery*
>*¼ cup French dressing*
>*2 hard-cooked eggs, chopped*
>*½ teaspoon onion salt*
>*⅛ teaspoon pepper*
>*6 frankfurter rolls*
>*Lettuce*

Combine salmon, celery, French dressing, eggs, and seasonings. Split 6 frankfurter rolls; line with lettuce; spoon salmon salad into rolls.

YIELD:　*6 servings.*

SALMON-MACARONI SWISS SALAD

8 ounces elbow macaroni
2 slices process Swiss cheese
Prepared mustard
2 cups torn spinach leaves
½ cup sliced radishes
2 small onions, thinly sliced
1 cup grated carrots
2 cans (8 ounces each) salmon, drained
French dressing

Cook macaroni in boiling salted water according to package directions. Drain and chill. Spread 1 slice of Swiss cheese with mustard. Top with remaining slice of cheese. Cut cheese into ½-inch squares. Combine macaroni, spinach, radishes, onions, and carrots. Break salmon into large pieces. Add salmon and cheese to macaroni mixture. Toss lightly but thoroughly. Chill. Just before serving, add enough French dressing to moisten. Toss lightly and serve.

YIELD:　*6 servings.*

SALMON-STUFFED FRENCH LOAF

1 can (1 pound) salmon
1 long, thin loaf French bread
1 package (3 ounces) cream cheese, mashed
3 tablespoons catchup

3 tablespoons mayonnaise
⅛ teaspoon pepper
¼ teaspoon dry mustard
3 tablespoons chopped pimiento
½ cup chopped sweet pickle
1 envelope unflavored gelatin
⅓ cup cold water

Drain and flake salmon. Cut French loaf in half and carefully remove the soft center, leaving a shell about ½ inch thick. Break soft bread removed from loaf into crumbs. Measure out 1½ cups crumbs for use. Combine salmon, measured crumbs, cream cheese, catchup, mayonnaise, pepper, mustard, pimiento, and pickle. Soften gelatin in cold water. Place over heat and stir until gelatin has dissolved. Add to salmon mixture; blend ingredients well. Fill each half of French loaf with mixture. Wrap the halves separately in plastic wrap. Store in the refrigerator for at least 8 hours. Serve in slices cut ½ inch thick.

YIELD: *About 24 slices.*

SALMON PATTIES

½ cup pastina
3 tablespoons butter or margarine
¼ cup minced onion
¼ cup chopped celery
2 cups canned or cooked flaked salmon
¼ cup minced parsley
1 egg, slightly beaten
1½ teaspoons salt
¼ teaspoon white pepper
Fine dry bread crumbs
⅓ cup fat or oil

Cook pastina as directed. Drain. Melt butter in saucepan; add onion and celery and cook until tender. Combine with pastina, salmon, parsley, egg, and seasonings. Mix thoroughly and shape into 8 patties. Coat on all sides with bread crumbs. Brown on both sides in hot fat in frying pan over moderate heat.

YIELD: *4 servings.*

SPANISH SALMON BAKE

1 cup elbow macaroni
1 can (1 pound) salmon, drained and flaked
1¼ cups shredded Cheddar cheese, divided
1½ cups corn flakes
1 cup milk
2 eggs, slightly beaten
¼ cup chopped pimiento
1 tablespoon chopped parsley
½ teaspoon finely chopped garlic
1 teaspoon salt
½ teaspoon pepper
½ cup packaged corn flake crumbs
1 tablespoon butter, melted
¼ teaspoon paprika

Cook macaroni in boiling salted water according to package directions. Combine with salmon, 1 cup of the cheese, corn flakes, milk, eggs, pimiento, parsley, garlic, salt, and pepper. Spread evenly in greased 10×6-inch baking dish. Combine corn flake crumbs with remaining cheese, butter, and paprika. Sprinkle over salmon mixture. Bake in a 350° F. oven about 40 minutes. Cut into 3×2½-inch pieces and serve, accompanied with Hot Tomato Sauce (below).

YIELD: *6 servings.*

HOT TOMATO SAUCE

2 tablespoons butter or margarine
½ cup finely chopped onion
½ cup finely chopped green pepper
1 teaspoon salt
½ teaspoon pepper
½ teaspoon chili powder
1 can (10¾ ounces) condensed tomato soup

Melt butter in saucepan; add onion and green pepper and cook until tender. Stir in salt, pepper, chili powder, and soup. Heat to serving temperature.

YIELD: 1¾ cups.

SALMON BAKE SUPREME

¼ cup butter or margarine
¼ cup flour
½ teaspoon salt
¼ teaspoon dried leaf thyme
⅛ teaspoon pepper
2 cups milk
2 packages (9 ounces each) frozen cut green beans,
    thawed†
1 can (1 pound) salmon, drained and flaked

Melt butter in a large saucepan; blend in flour, salt, thyme, and pepper. Remove from heat; stir in milk. Heat to boiling, stirring constantly. Boil and stir 1 minute. Stir in beans and salmon. Turn into a 1½-quart buttered casserole. Cover. Bake in a 400° F. oven 30 minutes.

YIELD: 5 to 6 servings.

† One pound fresh green beans, cooked and drained, may be substituted for frozen.

SALMON ROMANOFF

1 cup sour cream
2 cups cottage cheese
½ cup chopped green pepper
2 tablespoons flour
2 tablespoons minced onion
2 teaspoons Worcestershire sauce
½ teaspoon salt
1 clove garlic, crushed
Dash Tabasco
1 can (1 pound) salmon, drained and flaked
6 slices pineapple, drained
½ cup shredded Cheddar cheese

Combine sour cream, cottage cheese, green pepper, flour, onion, Worcestershire sauce, salt, garlic, and Tabasco. Stir in salmon. Butter 6 individual casseroles. Place about ¾ cup mixture in each; top with a pineapple slice. Bake in a 350° F. oven 15 to 20 minutes. Sprinkle Cheddar cheese over each pineapple slice.

YIELD: *6 servings.*

SAVORY SALMON ON SPAGHETTI

4 tablespoons butter or margarine
¼ cup finely chopped onion
1 cup sliced mushrooms
¼ cup flour
2 cups buttermilk
1 tablespoon chopped chives
2 tablespoons chopped parsley
½ teaspoon paprika
2 medium tomatoes, peeled and cut in eighths

2 cans (8 ounces each) salmon, drained and flaked
Salt
8 ounces spaghetti

Melt butter in saucepan; add onion and mushrooms and cook until tender, about 5 minutes. Blend in flour. Gradually add buttermilk and cook, stirring constantly, until mixture thickens and comes to a boil. Stir in chives, parsley, and paprika. Add tomatoes and salmon; season with salt to taste. Cook over low heat 10 minutes. Meanwhile, cook spaghetti in boiling salted water according to package directions; drain. Place on serving platter; spoon sauce over top.

YIELD: *4 to 6 servings.*

SHRIMP WITH NOODLES

1 can (10½ ounces) condensed cream of shrimp soup
⅓ cup water
½ cup sour cream
1 cup cooked shrimp
⅛ teaspoon paprika
2 cups cooked noodles

Combine soup and water in a saucepan; heat. Blend in sour cream. Add shrimp and paprika. Heat a few minutes; stirring occasionally. Serve over hot noodles.

YIELD: *4 servings.*

GALA SHRIMP PIE

1½ cups sifted all-purpose flour
½ teaspoon salt
½ cup shortening
½ cup shredded process American cheese
4 to 6 tablespoons cold water

Sift together flour and salt. Cut in shortening until mixture is
crumbly. Stir in cheese. Sprinkle with water, mixing lightly
until dough begins to stick together. Turn out on lightly
floured board or pastry cloth and press dough together. Reserve one third of dough. Roll out remaining dough to ⅛-inch
thickness. Fit into 9-inch pie pan. Trim and flute edge. Prick
with fork to allow steam to escape. Bake in 450° F. oven 15 to
18 minutes, or until lightly browned. Roll out reserved dough
to ⅛-inch thickness. Cut with floured cookie cutter or into
triangles. Place on ungreased baking sheet. Bake 10 to 12 minutes. Fill warm baked pastry shell with Shrimp Filling (below). Arrange cutouts on top of filling.

SHRIMP FILLING

½ cup butter or margarine
½ cup sifted all-purpose flour
½ teaspoon salt
¼ teaspoon pepper
1 cup chicken bouillon
1 cup milk
2 cups diced cooked shrimp
1½ cups seeded grape halves
1 can (4 ounces) button mushrooms, drained
½ cup chopped unblanched almonds
2 tablespoons prepared horseradish

Melt butter in saucepan. Blend in flour, salt, and pepper.
Combine bouillon and milk. Add liquid gradually to flour mixture, stirring constantly, until mixture thickens and comes to
a boil. Stir in shrimp, grapes, mushrooms, and almonds. Heat
to serving temperature. Stir in horseradish and immediately
turn into pie shell.

YIELD: *6 to 8 servings.*

SHRIMP IN AVOCADO HALVES

Prepare shrimp by cleaning it and cooking it 2 to 5 minutes in boiling water to which pickling spices have been added. (For each pound of shrimp, add 1 heaping teaspoon pickling spices to 1 quart of water.) Halve ripe avocados and carefully remove the seeds. Fill each half with 3 shrimp, and serve with Pimiento-Sour Cream Dressing (below).

YIELD: *4 servings.*

PIMIENTO-SOUR CREAM DRESSING

1 cup sour cream
½ teaspoon salt
1 tablespoon lemon juice
1 pimiento, diced

Combine ingredients and chill.

SEAFOOD AU GRATIN

1 can (11 ounces) condensed Cheddar cheese soup
¼ cup milk
2 cups cooked seafood (shrimp, lobster, crab, whitefish)
1 tablespoon chopped parsley
¼ cup buttered bread crumbs

Blend together soup and milk in a 1-quart casserole. Stir in seafood and parsley. Top with bread crumbs. Bake in a 400° F. oven 30 minutes.

YIELD: *3 or 4 servings.*

SEAFOOD SUPREME

1 tomato, chopped
1 cup mayonnaise or salad dressing
1 tablespoon chili sauce
½ teaspoon Worcestershire sauce
¼ teaspoon salt
⅛ teaspoon Tabasco
1 teaspoon each chopped chives, parsley, and dillweed
Salad greens
1½ pounds cooked, cleaned shrimp, lobster, and crab
*   meat*
Frozen French fried potatoes, cooked according to
*   package directions*
Onion or garlic salt

Combine tomato, mayonnaise, chili sauce, seasonings, chives, parsley, and dill; chill. At serving time, arrange greens in cocktail glass or on salad plate. Place the seafood on the greens and top with a generous amount of chilled sauce. Accompany the cocktail or salad with hot French fried potatoes, seasoned with onion or garlic salt.

YIELD: *6 to 8 servings.*

SWEET AND PUNGENT SHRIMP

1 can (9 ounces) pineapple slices
½ cup brown sugar
½ cup vinegar
2 tablespoons soy sauce
1¼ cups water, divided
3 tablespoons cornstarch
1 green pepper, cut in strips

1 tomato, cut into wedges
1 pound shrimp, cooked and cleaned

Drain syrup from pineapple into a saucepan. Cut pineapple slices in half and reserve. Add brown sugar, vinegar, soy sauce, and 1 cup water to pineapple syrup; bring to boil. Combine cornstarch and ¼ cup water; add to saucepan. Cook, stirring constantly, until thickened and clear. Add green pepper, pineapple, and tomato wedges. Cook 2 minutes. Add shrimp and cook to heat shrimp through.

YIELD: *4 servings.*

SHRIMP JAMBALAYA

2 pounds shrimp
¼ cup salad oil or butter
2 onions, chopped
1 clove garlic, minced
1 bay leaf, crumbled
2 cups uncooked rice
1 can (1 pound, 3 ounces) tomatoes
2 teaspoons salt
¼ teaspoon pepper
Lemon slices

Cook shrimp in boiling Court Bouillon (below) 2 to 5 minutes. Drain; reserve 1 cup court bouillon water. Shell and clean shrimp. Heat salad oil in very large skillet. Add onion, garlic, and bay leaf; cook until onion is tender and slightly browned. Add rice and cook, stirring constantly, until golden. Stir in reserved court bouillon water and tomatoes. Chop tomatoes with spoon. Add salt and pepper. Cover skillet and let cook 20 to 30 minutes, or until rice is cooked, and liquid absorbed. If mixture becomes too dry, add more water. Taste and season with more salt and pepper, if necessary. When rice is cooked, stir in shrimp, reserving some shrimp for garnishing. Garnish with extra shrimp and lemon slices.

YIELD: *6 to 8 servings.*

COURT BOUILLON

1½ quarts water
½ stalk celery
1 carrot, sliced
1 small onion, sliced
½ lemon, sliced
1 teaspoon salt
Few peppercorns

To water in large saucepan, add all ingredients. Bring water to boil. Let simmer for about 5 minutes.

SHRIMP CREOLE

¼ cup butter
1 cup coarsely chopped onions
1 cup chopped celery
1 small clove garlic, finely minced
2 tablespoons flour
1 teaspoon salt
1 teaspoon sugar
Dash cayenne
1 teaspoon paprika
½ small bay leaf
⅛ teaspoon Tabasco
½ cup diced green pepper
1 can (1 pound, 3 ounces) tomatoes (about 2¼ cups)
3 cups shrimp, cooked and cleaned

Melt butter in large skillet. Add onion, celery, and garlic and cook until tender. Blend in flour and seasonings; stir in green pepper and tomatoes. Cook 15 minutes, stirring occasionally. Add shrimp and heat to serving temperature. Serve with Cheese Rice (below).

YIELD: *6 servings.*

CHEESE RICE

1 tablespoon butter or margarine
1 teaspoon salt
1½ cups uncooked rice
3 cups boiling water
2 cups shredded American cheese
2 tablespoons finely chopped onion
1 teaspoon prepared mustard

Add butter, salt, and rice to boiling water. Bring to a boil; reduce heat to low. Cover and simmer until tender, about 20 to 25 minutes. Stir cheese, onion, and mustard into hot rice.

SHRIMP À LA KING

2 tablespoons butter or margarine
¼ cup chopped onion
1 cup (10¾ ounces) condensed cream of shrimp soup
¼ cup milk
1 cup diced cooked shrimp, cleaned
1 cup cooked peas
3 cups hot cooked noodles

Melt butter in saucepan; add onion and cook until tender. Add soup, milk, shrimp, and peas. Heat to serving temperature. Serve over noodles.

YIELD: *4 servings.*

GINGER BROILED LOBSTER TAILS

8 frozen lobster tails, thawed
¼ cup soy sauce
½ teaspoon ground ginger
¼ cup dry sherry

Snip out soft underside of shell to expose meat. Place tails meat-side up on broiling pan. Combine soy sauce, ginger, and sherry. Brush each tail with 1 tablespoon mixture. Place under broiler about 8 inches from source of heat; broil 10 to 12 minutes until tails are warm through and golden. Serve at once.

YIELD: *8 servings.*

LOBSTER MOUSSE

1 package (3 ounces) lemon-flavored gelatin
1 cup sour cream
3 tablespoons lemon juice
½ teaspoon salt
¼ teaspoon pepper
1 cup cut-up cooked lobster
½ cup mayonnaise
¼ cup chopped onion
½ cup chopped green pepper
⅔ cup wheat germ
2 tablespoons wine vinegar
½ teaspoon salt
1 teaspoon paprika
Lettuce
French dressing

Prepare gelatin according to package directions and refrigerate until thick and syrupy. Whip next 4 ingredients together and refrigerate. Combine remaining ingredients except lettuce and

French dressing, blending well, and refrigerate. Whip chilled gelatin until it stands in peaks, then fold in sour cream mixture and lobster salad mix. Turn into a 1½-quart ring mold and chill until firm. Cut in wedges and serve on lettuce leaf with French dressing.

YIELD: *6 servings.*

SHRIMP GUMBO

> *1 pound shrimp*
> *3 cups water*
> *1 stalk celery with top*
> *¼ teaspoon Tabasco*
> *2 teaspoons salt*
> *2 tablespoons butter*
> *1 clove garlic, minced*
> *1 large onion, chopped*
> *1 large green pepper, diced*
> *1 can (1 pound) tomatoes*
> *2 cups sliced fresh or frozen okra*
> *¼ teaspoon pepper*
> *½ teaspoon gumbo filé*
> *1 teaspoon sugar*
> *2 teaspoons chopped parsley*
> *¾ cup cooked rice*

Wash, peel, and devein shrimp, reserving shells. Combine shrimp shells, water, celery, Tabasco, and salt in 3-quart saucepan. Cover and simmer 20 minutes. Melt butter in skillet over moderate heat; add garlic, onion, and green pepper and cook 10 minutes, stirring frequently. Strain broth from shells and return to pan. Add garlic, onion, green pepper, tomatoes, and okra. Cover and simmer ½ hour. Add pepper, gumbo filé, sugar, and shrimp. Cover and simmer 10 minutes. Add parsley. Put 2 tablespoons rice in each soup plate; spoon in gumbo.

YIELD: *6 servings.*

SEAFOOD MARYLAND

1 can (10¾ ounces) condensed oyster stew
½ cup light cream
2 cups cut-up cooked seafood (lobster, shrimp, whitefish)
1 tablespoon chopped parsley
1 teaspoon lemon juice

Heat soup and cream in saucepan. Add seafood, parsley, and lemon juice. Heat to serving temperature. Serve over toast.

YIELD: *3 to 4 servings.*

LOBSTER SALAD

2 cups cut-up cooked lobster meat
½ cup chopped celery
1 hard-cooked egg, finely chopped
¼ cup mayonnaise or salad dressing
1 teaspoon curry powder
1 teaspoon lemon juice
Salt
Pepper
Salad greens

Mix lobster meat, celery, and egg. Add mayonnaise, curry, and lemon juice. Season with salt and pepper to taste. Serve on salad greens.

YIELD: *4 servings.*

LOBSTER TAILS DE JONGHE

4 (6 ounces each) rock-lobster tails
Salt

1⅓ cups fine dry bread crumbs
½ cup melted butter or margarine
1 clove garlic, crushed
¼ teaspoon salt
3 tablespoons chopped parsley
½ teaspoon dried leaf tarragon
⅓ cup dry sauterne or sherry

Cook rock-lobster tails in boiling salted water to cover. Cook
10 minutes; drain and cool in cold water. Remove undershell;
remove meat in 1 piece and drain well; coarsely chop meat.
Pat shells dry. Combine crumbs with melted butter, crushed
garlic, salt, parsley, tarragon, and 2 tablespoons of the wine.
Spoon half of crumb mixture into shells; top with lobster meat.
Spoon remaining crumbs over top. Sprinkle with half of remaining wine. Bake in a 400° F. oven 20 minutes or until
crumbs are golden and rock-lobster meat is heated through.
To serve, sprinkle with remaining wine.

YIELD: *4 servings.*

LOBSTER-SHRIMP THERMIDOR

1 tablespoon butter or margarine
1 cup sliced mushrooms
1 cup diced cooked lobster
1 cup cooked shrimp
1 can (10¾ ounces) condensed cream of shrimp soup
¼ cup milk
¼ teaspoon dry mustard
⅛ teaspoon cayenne
Grated Parmesan cheese
Paprika

Melt butter in saucepan. Add mushrooms, lobster, and shrimp;
cook until mushrooms are tender, about 5 minutes. Add soup;
blend in milk, dry mustard, and cayenne. Heat. Spoon mix-

ture into 3 individual baking dishes. Sprinkle cheese and paprika on top. Bake in a 400° F. oven about 15 minutes.

YIELD: *3 servings.*

FRENCH FRIED SHRIMP

1 cup sifted all-purpose flour
½ teaspoon salt
⅞ cup milk (1 cup minus 2 tablespoons)
1 egg white
2 pounds shrimp, cooked and cleaned
Oil for frying

Sift together flour and salt. Add milk and egg white; beat until smooth. Dip shrimp into batter, let excess batter drain off. Deep-fat fry at 385° F. about 3 minutes until golden brown. Drain on absorbent paper.

YIELD: *6 servings.*

CHEDDAR SHRIMP CASSEROLE

8 ounces macaroni
6 tablespoons butter
2 cups sliced mushrooms
1 teaspoon curry powder
1 teaspoon onion powder
2 tablespoons dry white wine
1 pint sour cream
1½ cups grated sharp Cheddar cheese, divided
2 cans (4½ ounces each) shrimp, drained
½ cup chopped scallions

Cook macaroni in boiling, salted water according to package directions. Drain well. Melt butter in a large skillet; add mushrooms and cook 5 minutes. Stir in curry and onion powder. Remove from heat; stir in wine. Blend in sour cream and 1 cup grated cheese. Add shrimp and scallions; mix well. Toss lightly with macaroni. Turn into a 1½-quart casserole. Sprinkle with remaining ½ cup cheese. Bake in 375° F. oven 25 to 30 minutes.

YIELD: *4 servings.*

MADRAS CURRY

¼ *cup peanut oil*
¼ *cup chopped mushrooms*
½ *cup chopped onion*
½ *cup diagonally sliced celery*
⅓ *cup flour*
2 *cups chicken broth*
1 *teaspoon Worcestershire sauce*
½ *teaspoon salt*
2 *teaspoons curry powder*
3 *cups cooked shrimp*
½ *cup raisins*
3 *cups hot cooked rice*

Heat peanut oil in skillet. Add mushrooms, onions, and celery; cook until lightly browned. Blend in flour. Add broth and cook, stirring constantly, until mixture thickens and comes to a boil. Stir in Worcestershire sauce, salt, and curry powder. Add shrimp and raisins; heat to serving temperature. Serve over rice.

YIELD: *6 servings.*

LOBSTER COPENHAGEN

2 packages (10 ounces each) frozen lobster tails
¼ cup butter
½ teaspoon onion powder
½ teaspoon dried dillweed
1 tablespoon lemon juice
Watercress
4 slices lemon

Remove lobster tails from wrappings. Plunge into boiling salted water; boil gently 5 minutes. Drain and run under cold water. Leaving shell on, cut tails into halves splitting straight down the middle lengthwise. Place on large broiler pan shell-side down. Melt butter; blend in onion powder, dillweed, and lemon juice. Brush tails with butter mixture. Place under broiler about 3 inches from source of heat. Broil 5 to 6 minutes until lobster meat is golden brown. To serve, arrange tails on a large serving platter garnished with watercress and lemon slices.

YIELD: *4 servings.*

SEAFOOD NEWBURG

2 tablespoons butter or margarine
2 tablespoons chopped onion
2 tablespoons diced green pepper
1 can (10¾ ounces) condensed oyster stew
½ cup milk
1 cup cut-up cooked lobster, crab meat, or shrimp
1 tablespoon dry sauterne
2 tablespoons diced pimiento
2 cups hot cooked rice

Melt butter in saucepan. Add onion and green pepper and cook until tender. Add soup; blend in milk. Heat to serving temperature. Add lobster, sauterne, and pimiento; heat 3 to 5 minutes longer. Serve over hot cooked rice.

YIELD: *4 servings.*

SPANISH-AMERICAN PAELLA

2 large onions, sliced
1 clove garlic
3 tomatoes, peeled and sliced
1 cup small black olives
⅓ cup olive oil
1½ cups uncooked rice
4 (6 ounces each) frozen rock-lobster tails
1 pound large shrimp
1 bay leaf
2 teaspoons salt
Stock, bouillon, or broth
1 tablespoon minced parsley
¼ teaspoon black pepper
1 dozen small clams, well scrubbed
1 can or jar (7 ounces) whole pimientos, drained

Sauté first 4 ingredients in hot olive oil in a metal paella pan or large ovenproof skillet. Push to one side of pan and add rice and brown. Combine lobster, shrimp, bay leaf, and salt in a large saucepan; add stock to cover. Bring to a boil; reduce heat and cook 10 minutes. Remove lobster and shrimp; add parsley and pepper to fish broth and pour this broth over contents of paella pan. Shell and clean fish; cut lobster into chunks, leave shrimp whole. Arrange shellfish, unopened clams, and large pieces of pimiento in paella pan. Add hot water, if necessary, so liquid level shows over rice. If using a paella pan or skillet without a lid, cover with heavy foil. Bake in a 350° F. oven 1 hour or more, until rice is cooked. Or cover and cook on top of range over low heat until rice is cooked. Garnish with additional pimientos just before serving.

YIELD: *6 to 8 servings.*

SEAFOOD POTATO PIE

2 tablespoons butter or margarine
½ cup diagonally sliced celery
2 tablespoons chopped onion
1 can (10¾ ounces) condensed oyster stew
½ cup milk
1 can (4½ ounces) shrimp, drained
1 can (6 ounces) lobster, drained
½ cup cooked peas
¼ teaspoon angostura bitters
¼ teaspoon dried leaf thyme
1 cup mashed potatoes
2 tablespoons shredded sharp cheese

Melt butter in saucepan. Add celery and onion and cook until tender. Add soup; blend in milk. Stir in shrimp, lobster, peas, bitters, and thyme. Heat. Pour into a 1½-quart casserole. Arrange potatoes around edge of casserole; sprinkle with cheese. Bake in 450° F. oven 15 minutes or until potatoes are browned.

YIELD: *4 servings.*

FISHERMAN'S PIE

2 tablespoons butter or margarine
1 medium onion, finely chopped
¼ cup finely chopped green pepper

3 tablespoons flour
2 cans (4 ounces each) sliced mushrooms
Milk
1 cup shredded process American cheese, divided
2 cans (7¾ ounces each) crab meat
3 hard-cooked eggs, chopped
Salt
Pepper
2 cups seasoned mashed potatoes

Melt butter in saucepan; add onion and green pepper and cook until tender. Blend in flour. Drain mushrooms. Add enough milk to mushroom liquid to make 2 cups. Reserve. Gradually add reserved milk mixture and cook, stirring constantly, until mixture thickens and comes to a boil. Add ½ cup cheese and stir until cheese is melted. Add crab meat. Arrange alternate layers of cheese sauce, eggs, and mushrooms in a greased 2-quart casserole. Season with salt and pepper. Combine potatoes with remaining ½ cup cheese. Spoon potato mixture around edge of casserole. Bake in a 350° F. oven 30 to 40 minutes.

YIELD: *6 servings.*

FLAVORSOME MACARONI-CRAB SALAD
WITH PINEAPPLE-CREAM DRESSING

8 ounces elbow macaroni
1 can (1 pound, 4 ounces) crushed pineapple
1 can (7¾ ounces) crab meat
½ cup finely chopped celery
3 egg yolks
½ cup sugar
2 tablespoons lemon juice
1 teaspoon grated lemon rind
Dash salt
½ cup heavy cream, whipped

Cook macaroni in boiling salted water according to package directions. Drain and chill. Drain pineapple and reserve ½ cup pineapple syrup. Flake crab meat in large pieces. Combine macaroni, pineapple, crab meat and celery; mix lightly. Chill. Beat egg yolks and sugar together in top of double boiler. Add lemon juice, lemon rind, pineapple syrup, and dash salt; mix well. Cook over boiling water until mixture thickens and coats spoon, stirring occasionally. Cool. Fold in whipped cream; chill. Add dressing to salad. Mix lightly.

YIELD: *4 to 6 servings.*

SEAFOOD BAKE

1 can (10¾ ounces) condensed cream of mushroom soup
⅓ cup salad dressing
⅓ cup milk
1 can (4½ ounces) shrimp, drained
1 can (7¾ ounces) crab meat
1 can (5 ounces) water chestnuts, drained and sliced
1 cup finely chopped celery
2 tablespoons chopped parsley
2 teaspoons grated onion
2 cups cooked macaroni

Combine soup, salad dressing, and milk in a 1½-quart casserole. Stir in remaining ingredients. Bake in a 350° F. oven 30 minutes.

YIELD: *4 to 6 servings.*

SHRIMP CHOW MEIN

2 tablespoons butter or margarine
¾ cup sliced mushrooms

1 cup sliced onion
3 cups sliced celery
¼ cup soy sauce
2 cups water, divided
3 vegetable bouillon cubes
¼ cup cornstarch
1 pound shrimp, cooked and cleaned
Chow mein noodles

Melt butter in large skillet. Add mushrooms, onions, and celery. Cook over medium heat until vegetables are partially tender, about 5 minutes. Add soy sauce, 1¾ cups water, and bouillon cubes; cover and simmer until vegetables are just tender, about 10 minutes. Mix cornstarch and remaining water to make a smooth paste; stir into vegetable mixture. Cook, stirring constantly, until mixture is thickened and clear. Add shrimp; heat to serving temperature. Serve on chow mein noodles.

YIELD: *4 servings.*

SHRIMP CURRY

2 tablespoons butter or margarine
2 small onions, chopped
1 clove garlic, minced
2 tablespoons curry powder
½ teaspoon salt
1 can (8 ounces) tomato sauce
1 cup chicken broth
3 tablespoons lemon juice
½ cup light cream
2 pounds shrimp, cooked and cleaned
3 cups hot cooked rice
2 tablespoons toasted almonds

Melt butter in a saucepan. Add onions and garlic and cook until tender. Blend in curry powder and salt. Add tomato sauce and chicken broth. Cook over low heat, stirring occasionally, about 30 minutes. Stir in lemon juice, then cream. Add shrimp and heat through. Serve over hot rice, garnished with toasted almonds. If desired, serve little dishes of chutney, coconut, and raisins.

YIELD: 6 servings.

TEMPURA

24 large shrimp, shelled and deveined
Oil for frying

BATTER:

1 egg
⅔ cup water
½ teaspoon salt
½ teaspoon Ac'cent
¼ teaspoon Tabasco
1 cup flour

SAUCE:

½ cup beef bouillon
¼ cup soy sauce
2 teaspoons sugar
¼ teaspoon Tabasco
¼ teaspoon Ac'cent
Horseradish, radishes and ginger

Slit undersection of shrimp to prevent excessive curling. Wash and dry thoroughly. Fill heavy kettle or deep-fat fryer at least three quarters full with oil; heat until temperature reaches

375° F. Beat egg lightly with fork or wire whisk; add water, salt, Ac'cent, and Tabasco. Continue beating and add flour. Batter should be smooth. Dip shrimp into batter; drop into hot oil. Fry until golden brown. Drain and serve hot with warmed sauce.

Combine bouillon, soy sauce, sugar, Tabasco, and Ac'cent in saucepan. Heat and pour into 4 small bowls, together with separate bowls of horseradish, radishes, and ginger.

YIELD: *4 servings.*

Note: If desired, sliced raw vegetables (green beans, eggplant, carrots, green pepper) may be dipped in batter and fried.

SEAFOOD CASHEW CASSEROLE

1 package (9 ounces) frozen lobster tails
1 package (6 ounces) frozen crab meat, thawed and
    drained
¼ cup butter or margarine
1 cup chopped celery
¼ cup chopped onion
¼ cup chopped green pepper
½ cup water
2 tablespoons milk
2 tablespoons cornstarch
1 tablespoon soy sauce
⅛ teaspoon Tabasco
1 cup sour cream
1 can (3 ounces) chow mein noodles
⅓ cup coarsely chopped cashew nuts

Cook lobster according to package directions; remove meat from shells and cut into chunks. Set seafood aside. Melt butter in a skillet; add celery, onion, and green pepper and cook until tender. Combine water, milk, cornstarch, soy sauce, and Tabasco; stir into skillet. Cook over low heat, stirring constantly, until thickened. Stir in sour cream. Remove from heat. Add lobster and crab meat. Turn into 1½-quart buttered casserole; sprinkle noodles and nuts over top. Bake in a 350° F. oven 30 to 40 minutes.

YIELD: *4 to 6 servings.*

SEAFOOD KABOBS

> *⅓ cup salad oil*
> *3 tablespoons lemon juice*
> *1 clove garlic, halved*
> *½ teaspoon salt*
> *2 tablespoons chili sauce*
> *1 tablespoon soy sauce*
> *1 pound large shrimp*
> *½ pound scallops*
> *2 rock-lobster tails*
> *Buttered rice*
> *Diced pimiento*

Combine oil with lemon juice, garlic, salt, chili and soy sauces; let stand. Shell and devein shrimp. Halve scallops. Cut away undershells of rock-lobster tails with kitchen scissors; then *carefully* insert fingers between shell and raw rock-lobster tail meat and work out meat from shell. Cut each lobster tail into 3 sections. Alternate seafood on skewers. Place kabobs in shallow dish and pour marinade over them; let stand ½ to 3 hours. Remove skewers from marinade and broil until done, about 5 minutes on each side. Serve with buttered rice that has been tossed with diced pimiento.

YIELD: *6 servings.*

THREE-WAY FISH PIE

1 small onion
1 carrot
1 stalk celery
Salt
Pepper
1 quart water
1½ pounds halibut or flounder
1 chicken bouillon cube
2 tablespoons butter or margarine
1 tablespoon chopped onion
2 tablespoons flour
1 teaspoon chopped parsley
½ pound cooked shrimp
½ pound cooked scallops
Pastry for single-crust pie

Boil whole onion, carrot, celery, salt, and pepper in 1 quart water. After boiling 10 minutes, add fish, cover and simmer until tender. Remove skin and bones; set fish aside. Return bones and skin to the bouillon; cook 15 minutes longer, then add the bouillon cube. Strain and reserve this stock. Melt butter in a saucepan. Add onion and cook until tender. Blend in flour. Gradually add 2¼ cups of the strained stock. Cook, stirring occasionally, until mixture thickens and comes to a boil. Add parsley and season to taste with salt and pepper. Break fish in large pieces and place in a deep greased baking dish, alternating with the boiled shrimp and scallops. Pour the sauce over all and cover with pastry. Make several incisions in crust. Bake in a 450° F. oven 12 minutes, then reduce heat to 350° F. and bake 20 minutes longer.

YIELD: *6 servings.*

SEAFOOD RAREBIT

2 tablespoons butter or margarine
¼ cup chopped green pepper
4 cups shredded sharp Cheddar cheese
1 tablespoon flour
½ teaspoon dry mustard
½ teaspoon Worcestershire sauce
1 egg, slightly beaten
¾ cup tomato juice
1 cup chopped cooked lobster or shrimp
4 English muffins, split and toasted

In top of double boiler melt butter; add green pepper and cook until tender. Place over hot water; add cheese and heat, stirring occasionally, until cheese is melted. Stir in flour, mustard, and Worcestershire sauce. Combine egg and juice; stir into cheese. Add lobster. Cook until thick, stirring frequently. Serve on English muffins.

YIELD: 4 servings.

LOBSTER CANTONESE

2 tablespoons peanut oil
1½ teaspoons salt
⅛ teaspoon pepper
1 tablespoon finely diced carrot
1 tablespoon finely diced celery
1 tablespoon finely diced scallion
1 can (6 ounces) lobster
1 cup chicken bouillon
1 egg, slightly beaten
2 tablespoons cornstarch

2 teaspoons soy sauce
¼ cup water
2 cups hot cooked rice

Heat peanut oil in a large heavy skillet. Combine salt, pepper, carrot, celery, scallion, and lobster. Add to skillet with chicken bouillon. Cover pan tightly and cook over moderate heat about 10 minutes. Add egg and cook over high heat for 2 minutes, stirring constantly. Blend together and add cornstarch, soy sauce, and water. Cook for a few more minutes, stirring constantly, until mixture thickens. Serve over hot cooked rice.

YIELD: *4 servings.*

SCALLOPS PARISIENNE

2 tablespoons butter or margarine
2 tablespoons chopped onion
½ cup sliced mushrooms
1 pound scallops
1 can (10¾ ounces) condensed cream of shrimp soup
⅓ cup milk
2 teaspoons lemon juice
⅛ teaspoon pepper
¼ teaspoon dried leaf thyme
½ cup buttered bread crumbs

Melt butter in saucepan. Add onion and mushrooms and cook until tender. Add scallops; cook 5 minutes. Place scallops in shallow baking dish. Combine soup, milk, lemon juice, and seasonings; pour over scallops. Top with crumbs. Bake in a 350° F. oven 30 minutes.

YIELD: *3 to 4 servings.*

SCALLOPS NEWBURG

1 pound scallops
1 quart boiling water
¼ cup butter or margarine
1 can (8 ounces) sliced mushrooms; drain and reserve
    liquid
Water
1 clove garlic, peeled and split
3 tablespoons flour
1 cup instant nonfat dry milk
¾ teaspoon salt
2 egg yolks, beaten
¼ cup chopped pimiento
1 tablespoon lemon juice
Dash cayenne
4 toast cups

Cut scallops in half. Place in boiling salted water. Cover and
return to the boiling point. Simmer 5 minutes; drain. Melt
butter in a saucepan or chafing dish. Add enough water to
mushroom liquid to make 2 cups. Reserve. Add garlic and
drained mushrooms to saucepan; sauté about 1 minute. Discard garlic and blend in flour. Cool. Mix nonfat dry milk,
salt, and mushroom liquid. Blend into flour mixture. Cook,
stirring constantly, until mixture thickens and comes to a boil.
Add small portion to beaten egg yolks, then return to mixture
and cook about 1 minute. Stir in scallops, pimiento, lemon
juice, and cayenne pepper. Serve in toast cups.

YIELD: *4 servings.*

SCALLOPED OYSTERS AND CLAMS

1⅓ cups packaged seasoned bread dressing
⅓ cup melted butter or margarine
3 hard-cooked eggs, chopped
1 can (8 ounces) oysters
1 can (8 ounces) minced clams
1 can (10¾ ounces) condensed cream of mushroom soup
1 tablespoon minced onion
2 tablespoons chopped parsley

Mix bread dressing with butter; reserve ⅓ cup of the mixture. Combine remaining dressing with the chopped eggs, ¾ cup liquid drained from oysters and clams, drained oysters and clams, soup, onion, and parsley. Put in a shallow baking dish and sprinkle with reserved dressing. Bake in a 400° F. oven about 20 minutes.

YIELD: *4 to 6 servings.*

SEA SCALLOPS TROPICAL

¼ cup lime juice
½ teaspoon salt
⅛ teaspoon ground ginger
2 tablespoons soy sauce
1 pound scallops
1 egg, well beaten
1 cup fine dry bread crumbs
⅓ cup grated or flaked coconut
1 teaspoon curry powder
Oil for deep-drying

Combine lime juice, salt, ginger, and soy sauce. Pour over scallops in small bowl and let stand 1 to 3 hours in refrigerator.

Drain. Pour egg over scallops and toss to coat thoroughly. Combine crumbs, coconut, and curry in clean paper bag. Add scallops. Shake to coat thoroughly. Deep-fry in oil heated to 375° F. for 2 to 3 minutes or until golden brown.

YIELD: *4 servings.*

FRIED CLAM CAKES

2 cups sifted all-purpose flour
1 teaspoon baking powder
½ teaspoon salt
1 pint clams
2 eggs, well beaten
1 cup milk
Oil for deep-frying

Sift together flour, baking powder, and salt. Drain clams; measure ½ cup liquid. Using the fine blade, grind clams in a food chopper; reserve. Add eggs, clam liquid, and milk to sifted ingredients; mix well. Stir in clams. Drop by large spoonfuls into hot, deep fat. When nicely browned, remove from pan and drain. Serve while hot.

YIELD: *4 servings.*

"BEST EVER" FRIED CLAMS

1 egg, separated
½ cup milk, divided
3 teaspoons melted butter or margarine, divided
¼ teaspoon salt
½ cup sifted flour
24 clams, drained and cleaned
Oil for deep-frying
Chili sauce

Beat the egg yolk; add ¼ cup milk and 1½ teaspoons butter. Sift together salt and flour; stir into yolk mixture and beat until smooth. Add remaining ¼ cup milk and butter, then fold in the stiffly beaten egg white. Dip each clam into the fritter batter and fry in deep fat heated to 375° F. until golden brown, turning frequently. Drain on absorbent paper. Serve with chili sauce.

YIELD: *4 servings.*

COTTAGE CLAMBAKE EN CASSEROLE

3 cups cooked rice
¼ cup butter or margarine
¼ cup flour
2 cups milk
1 teaspoon salt
½ teaspoon garlic salt
⅛ teaspoon Tabasco
½ teaspoon Worcestershire sauce
¼ cup grated onion
1½ teaspoons lemon juice
2 cans (8 ounces each) minced clams, well drained
3 cups cottage cheese
1 tablespoon chopped parsley
2 tablespoons fine dry bread crumbs
6 stuffed olives, sliced

Place rice in a 2-quart casserole. Melt butter in a heavy saucepan. Blend in flour. Gradually add milk and cook, stirring constantly, until mixture thickens and comes to a boil. Add salt, garlic salt, Tabasco, Worcestershire sauce, onion, and lemon juice. Stir in clams; blend well. Remove from heat and fold in cottage cheese. Stir in parsley. Pour over rice in casserole. Sprinkle bread crumbs over top. Bake in 350° F. oven 30 minutes. Garnish with stuffed olive slices just before serving.

YIELD: *6 servings.*

CLAM 'N' CORN BAKE

2 cans (6½ ounces each) minced clams
1 cup diced raw potato
1 cup drained whole-kernel corn
2 tablespoons minced onion
½ cup light cream
1 teaspoon dried leaf tarragon
¼ teaspoon pepper
1 cup fine cracker crumbs
2 tablespoons melted butter
2 tablespoons chopped parsley

Drain liquid from clams and add to potato cubes; cook potatoes until just tender, about 10 minutes. Combine clams, potatoes, and corn; turn into a 1½-quart casserole. Sprinkle with onion. Combine cream, tarragon, and pepper; pour into casserole. Mix cracker crumbs with melted butter and spread over the clam mixture. Sprinkle with parsley. Bake in 350° F. oven 25 to 30 minutes.

YIELD: 3 servings.

MUSSEL STEW

6 medium onions, chopped
3 tablespoons butter or margarine, divided
3 cups mussel liquid
4 tablespoons flour
2 cups scalded milk
1 quart mussel meat
½ teaspoon salt
Dash cayenne

1 egg yolk, slightly beaten
1 tablespoon minced pimiento

Cook onions slowly in 2 tablespoons of the butter in a deep saucepan about 5 minutes. Add mussel liquid, cover and cook 30 minutes. Press mixture through a sieve. Melt remaining tablespoon butter in a deep saucepan. Make a paste of the flour by stirring it smooth in a little of the warm milk, using a separate bowl. Gradually add remaining milk, stirring well. Add this mixture, with the mussel meat and seasonings, to the melted butter. Cook and stir steadily over low heat 5 minutes. Add the sieved mixture to the cream sauce, then rapidly stir in egg yolk and pimiento. Reheat about 1 minute.

YIELD: *6 servings.*

FRENCH FRIED MUSSELS

12 saltines
1 tablespoon butter or margarine
1 pound mussels, opened and cleaned
Salt
Pepper
Flour
1 egg
1 tablespoon water
Oil for deep-frying

Put saltines in oven with a small piece of butter on each and toast to a light brown. When cool, roll them finely, then sift. Wash mussels; dry. Sprinkle with salt and pepper and roll in flour. Dip in egg beaten lightly with water, then in sifted cracker crumbs. Fry in deep fat heated to 375° F. Drain on soft paper.

YIELD: *6 servings.*

OYSTERS LUCERNE

1 package (10 ounces) frozen chopped spinach
2 tablespoons butter or margarine
1 teaspoon onion salt
¼ teaspoon hot mustard
¼ teaspoon dried leaf oregano
⅛ teaspoon nutmeg
1 cup light cream
1 cup grated Swiss cheese, divided
2 eggs, lightly beaten
12 oysters

Cook spinach according to package directions; drain well.
Melt butter in saucepan. Blend in onion salt, mustard, oregano,
nutmeg, and cream. Cook, stirring constantly, until mixture
thickens and comes to a boil. Blend in ½ cup cheese until
smooth. Add a little hot mixture to beaten eggs; return to
saucepan. Cook until mixture thickens slightly. Stir half the
sauce into drained spinach. Blend remaining ½ cup cheese
into the rest of cream mixture until smooth. Spoon spinach
into 12 shells or individual casseroles. Place 1 oyster on each
spinach bed. Spoon cheese sauce over oysters. Place under
broiler 5 to 10 minutes until cheese bubbles and browns. Serve
hot.

YIELD: 4 servings.

OYSTER CASSEROLE

½ cup pastina
2 tablespoons butter or margarine
¼ cup chopped onion

2 tablespoons flour
1 pint oysters
1 cup milk
1 teaspoon salt
¼ teaspoon dried leaf marjoram
2 cups diced cooked celery
½ cup buttered bread crumbs

Cook pastina according to package directions; drain. Melt butter in saucepan, saute onions; blend in flour. Drain oysters; reserve ¼ cup liquid. Add oyster liquid to saucepan with milk, salt, and marjoram. Cook, stirring constantly, until mixture thickens and comes to a boil. Remove from heat; stir in pastina and celery. In a greased 1½-quart casserole, place one third of the pastina mixture. Add half the oysters and a second layer of pastina. Add remaining oysters and top with rest of pastina. Sprinkle with crumbs. Bake in a 425° F. oven 30 minutes or until thoroughly hot and crumbs are golden brown.

YIELD: *4 to 6 servings.*

FRIED OYSTERS WITH LEMON BUTTER

1 pint oysters
1 egg, beaten
1 tablespoon milk
¼ teaspoon salt
Dash pepper
½ cup corn meal, dry bread crumbs, or cracker crumbs
1 cup salad oil
¼ cup melted butter or margarine
1 teaspoon grated lemon rind
2 tablespoons lemon juice
⅛ teaspoon dried leaf marjoram
Parsley

Drain oysters. Combine egg, milk, salt, and pepper. Dip oysters
in egg mixture; roll in corn meal. Fry in hot oil 2 to 3 minutes
on each side until browned. Drain on absorbent paper. Combine butter, lemon rind and juice, and marjoram. Serve hot
with fried oysters. Garnish with parsley.

YIELD: *4 servings.*

OYSTERS À LA QUEEN

> *2 tablespoons butter or margarine*
> *¼ cup minced onion*
> *2 tablespoons flour*
> *1 can (10½ ounces) condensed oyster stew*
> *¼ cup milk*
> *2 tablespoons diced pimiento*
> *1 can (4 ounces) sliced mushrooms, drained*
> *4 slices buttered toast*

Melt butter in saucepan; add onion and cook until tender.
Blend in flour. Stir in oyster stew, milk, and pimiento and
mushrooms. Heat to serving temperature. Serve over toast.

YIELD: *3 to 4 servings.*

CHINESE FRIED FISH

> *¼ cup salad oil*
> *2 tablespoons chopped green pepper*
> *1 can (6½ or 7 ounces) tuna, drained*
> *1 cup cooked rice*
> *2 hard-cooked eggs, chopped*
> *1 tablespoon soy sauce*
> *¼ teaspoon salt*
> *Parsley*

Heat oil in a medium skillet; add green pepper and cook until tender. Add remaining ingredients except parsley. Stir over medium heat for 5 minutes until thoroughly heated. Garnish with parsley.

YIELD: *3 to 4 servings.*

TUNA TERRIFIC

*1 package (6 ounces) seasoned long grain and wild
    rice
1 package (10 ounces) frozen peas
4 egg yolks, slightly beaten
1 can (10¾ ounces) condensed cream of mushroom soup
¾ cup milk
2 cans (9¼ ounces each) tuna, drained and flaked
¾ cup thinly sliced celery
¾ cup thinly sliced carrot
1 can (4 ounces) mushroom stems and pieces, drained
½ teaspoon dried dillweed
4 egg whites
¼ teaspoon cream of tartar*

Prepare rice according to package directions. Stir in frozen peas; remove from heat. Combine egg yolks, soup, and milk. Stir in tuna, celery, carrot, mushrooms, and dillweed. Stir in rice. Beat egg whites until frothy. Add cream of tartar and beat until stiff but not dry; fold into rice mixture. Divide into 2 buttered 1½-quart casseroles. Bake in a 375° F. oven 40 to 45 minutes or until a knife inserted near center comes out clean. Let stand 5 minutes before serving. Serve with Parsley Sauce (below).

PARSLEY SAUCE

¼ cup butter
¼ cup flour
½ teaspoon salt
2½ cups milk
2 tablespoons chopped parsley
¾ teaspoon grated lemon rind

Melt butter in saucepan; blend in flour and salt. Remove from heat; stir in milk. Heat to boiling, stirring constantly. Boil and stir 1 minute. Stir in parsley and lemon rind. Serve with casseroles.

YIELD: *6 servings.*

TUNA, CHEESE, AND CAULIFLOWER CASSEROLE

1 medium cauliflower
1 can (6½ or 7 ounces) tuna
1 tablespoon butter or margarine
4 tablespoons flour
2 cups milk
¾ cup grated process American cheese, divided
½ cup chopped celery
1 teaspoon salt
Dash onion salt
¼ teaspoon pepper
Paprika

Soak cauliflower, head down, in cold salted water 20 minutes. Separate into flowerets. Cook, covered, in boiling salted water about 10 minutes, or until tender. Drain. Place cauliflower in bottom of greased 1½-quart casserole. Drain tuna and reserve oil; break tuna into pieces. Heat tuna oil with butter in saucepan over low heat; blend in flour. Gradually add milk and cook, stirring constantly, until mixture thickens and comes to a boil. Add ½ cup cheese and stir until cheese is melted. Add celery, salt, onion salt, pepper, and tuna. Pour over cauliflower; sprinkle with remaining cheese. Dust with paprika. Bake in 375° F. oven 30 minutes.

YIELD: *4 servings.*

SPANISH TUNA SAUCE AND EGGS

> *2 tablespoons butter or margarine*
> *1 medium onion, chopped*
> *1 tablespoon flour*
> *1 can (1 pound, 4 ounces) tomatoes*
> *1 medium green pepper, chopped*
> *1 cup chopped celery*
> *1 teaspoon salt*
> *⅛ teaspoon pepper*
> *1 can (6½ or 7 ounces) tuna, drained and flaked*
> *4 hard-cooked eggs*

Melt butter in saucepan; add onion and cook until tender. Blend in flour. Add tomatoes, green pepper, celery, salt, pepper, and tuna. Cover and cook over low heat 20 minutes, stirring occasionally. Cut eggs in half lengthwise and arrange on serving dish. Pour tuna sauce over eggs.

YIELD: *6 servings.*

SPAGHETTI WITH PICKLE-TUNA SAUCE

8 ounces spaghetti
¼ cup butter or margarine
¼ cup flour
2 cups milk
¼ cup drained prepared horseradish
2 tablespoons finely chopped sweet cucumber pickles
1 can (6½ or 7 ounces) tuna, drained and flaked
Salt
Pepper
Paprika

Cook spaghetti in boiling salted water according to package directions; drain. Meanwhile, melt butter in saucepan; blend in flour. Gradually add milk and cook, stirring constantly, until mixture thickens and comes to a boil. Add horseradish, pickles, and tuna; mix well. Season with salt and pepper. Heat to serving temperature, stirring occasionally. Serve over spaghetti and sprinkle with paprika.

YIELD: *4 to 6 servings.*

TUNA SCOTCH IN CHAFING DISH

1 chicken bouillon cube
½ cup boiling water
4 egg yolks
¼ cup dry sherry
1 tablespoon chopped parsley
1 tablespoon finely chopped onion
1 cup heavy cream
Dash cayenne
½ teaspoon paprika
Salt
Pepper

1 can (6½ or 7 ounces) tuna, drained
1 can (6 ounces) whole mushrooms, drained
Buttered toast

Dissolve bouillon cube in boiling water in top of chafing dish. Beat egg yolks and sherry together; add parsley and onion. Add a little of hot bouillon to egg yolks; mix well and add to remaining hot bouillon. Heat to boiling point over direct heat, stirring constantly. Place over hot water pan; add cream and seasonings. Cook 3 minutes, stirring constantly. Break tuna into large pieces and add to sauce with mushrooms; heat thoroughly. Serve over toast.

YIELD: *4 to 6 servings.*

TUNA AND BAVARIAN RED CABBAGE

2 tablespoons butter or margarine
1 medium head red cabbage, shredded
1½ teaspoons salt, divided
⅛ teaspoon pepper
1 tablespoon sugar
2 tablespoons vinegar
1 can (6½ or 7 ounces) tuna, drained
1 cup sour cream
Dash nutmeg
Paprika

Melt butter in large skillet. Add cabbage, 1 teaspoon of the salt, pepper, sugar, and vinegar. Cover and cook over medium heat until cabbage is almost tender, about 10 minutes. Break tuna into pieces and add to cabbage mixture; cook 5 minutes. Meanwhile, beat sour cream until light and fluffy; add remaining ½ teaspoon salt and nutmeg and mix well. Serve cabbage-tuna mixture topped with sour cream and sprinkled lightly with paprika.

YIELD: *4 servings.*

SCALLOPED MACARONI, TUNA, AND WALNUT CASSEROLE

8 ounces elbow macaroni
⅓ cup butter or margarine
⅓ cup flour
3 cups milk
1 can (6½ or 7 ounces) tuna, drained and flaked
⅔ cup coarsely chopped walnuts
3 hard-cooked eggs, chopped
1¼ teaspoons salt
½ teaspoon dry mustard
⅛ teaspoon dried leaf thyme
¼ teaspoon pepper
2 tablespoons finely chopped walnuts
2 tablespoons butter or margarine

Cook macaroni in boiling salted water according to package directions. While macaroni is cooking, melt ⅓ cup butter in saucepan; blend in flour. Gradually add milk and cook, stirring constantly until mixture thickens and comes to a boil. Combine macaroni and sauce. Add tuna to macaroni mixture with ⅔ cup walnuts, eggs, salt, mustard, thyme, and pepper; mix thoroughly. Turn into a greased 2-quart casserole. Top with 2 tablespoons walnuts and dot with 2 tablespoons butter. Bake in a 350° F. oven 30 minutes.

YIELD: *4 to 6 servings.*

ONE-DISH TUNA DINNER

14 small white onions, peeled
1 teaspoon salt
2 tablespoons butter or margarine

    1½ cups milk
    1 package (10 ounces) frozen peas
    3 tablespoons flour
    ¼ cup cold water
    1 can (6½ or 7 ounces) tuna, drained
    1 cup packaged biscuit mix
    ⅓ cup milk

Combine onions, salt, butter in saucepan with enough water to cover onions. Cook, covered, over medium heat until onions are tender. Add 1½ cups milk and peas. Heat to boiling point. Combine flour and ¼ cup water; blend. Add to onion mixture and cook, stirring constantly, until thickened. Break tuna into large pieces and add to onion mixture. Turn into greased 1½-quart casserole. Combine biscuit mix and ⅓ cup milk; mix well. Turn out on lightly floured surface and knead 10 times. Roll out to ½-inch thickness and cut into 4 rounds. Place biscuit rounds over tuna mixture. Bake in a 450° F. oven for 20 minutes or until biscuits are done.

YIELD: *4 servings.*

POT-LUCKY TUNA

    3 tablespoons butter or margarine
    2 tablespoons chopped onion
    ¼ cup chopped celery
    3 tablespoons flour
    ½ teaspoon salt
    ¼ teaspoon pepper
    1 can (8 ounces) peas and carrots
    1¼ cups milk
    1½ cups shredded Cheddar cheese
    1 can (6½ or 7 ounces) tuna, drained and flaked
    1 package refrigerated biscuits

Melt butter in a saucepan; add onion and celery and cook until tender. Blend in flour, salt, and pepper. Drain vegetables; add liquid to milk. Gradually add milk mixture to saucepan and cook, stirring constantly, until mixture thickens and comes to a boil. Add cheese; stir until melted. Add tuna and drained vegetables. Turn into a 1½-quart casserole. Top with biscuits; bake in a 350° F. oven 25 minutes.

YIELD: *4 servings.*

CASSEROLE OF TUNA FISH

8 ounces noodles
¼ cup butter or margarine
2 tablespoons flour
2 cups milk
2 tablespoons diced pimiento
2 tablespoons diced green pepper
2 tablespoons chopped onion
1½ cups diced, cooked carrots
1 small head cooked cauliflower
1 can (6½ or 7 ounces) tuna, drained

Cook noodles in boiling salted water according to package directions. Melt butter in saucepan; blend in flour. Gradually add milk and cook, stirring constantly, until mixture thickens and comes to a boil. Stir in pimiento, green pepper, onion, carrots, and cauliflower flowerets. Place a layer of cooked, drained noodles in a buttered casserole; arrange half of vegetable mixture over top, then place fish in center. Add remaining sauce and top with noodles. Bake in a 350° F. oven 30 minutes.

YIELD: *6 servings.*

TUNA-CORN PUDDING

1½ cups wheat germ
¼ cup melted butter or margarine
1 can (12 ounces) whole-kernel corn, drained
2 cans (6½ or 7 ounces each) tuna, drained and flaked
1 teaspoon lemon juice
1⅓ cups milk
2 eggs, beaten
¾ teaspoon salt
2 hard-cooked eggs, sliced

Combine wheat germ and melted butter or margarine. Place half of buttered wheat germ in greased 1½-quart casserole. Add corn, then top with tuna. Sprinkle with lemon juice. Combine milk, eggs, and salt; pour over tuna. Top with remaining buttered wheat germ mixture. Bake in a 350° F. oven 1 hour. Garnish top of casserole with sliced eggs.

YIELD: 6 servings.

TUNA-BROCCOLI ALMONDINE

2 packages (10 ounces each) frozen broccoli
2 cans (6½ or 7 ounces each) tuna, drained and flaked
½ cup slivered almonds
¼ cup butter or margarine
¼ cup flour
½ teaspoon salt
⅛ teaspoon pepper
⅛ teaspoon nutmeg
2 cups milk
1 tablespoon dry sherry, optional
Paprika

Cook broccoli until tender; drain and arrange in buttered 10×6×1¾-inch baking dish. Spread tuna evenly over broccoli. Sauté almonds in butter in saucepan until lightly browned; remove from butter and drain on paper towels. Blend flour, salt, pepper, and nutmeg into butter. Add milk and cook, stirring constantly, until mixture thickens and comes to a boil. Stir sherry into sauce and pour over tuna. Sprinkle with paprika. Bake in 350° F. oven 25 minutes. Sprinkle almonds over top just before serving.

YIELD: 6 servings.

GERMAN GREEN BEANS AND TUNA

3 tablespoons butter or margarine
2 tablespoons flour
1 teaspoon salt
1 cup water
1 teaspoon grated onion
1 package (9 ounces) frozen green beans
1 can (6½ or 7 ounces) tuna, drained and flaked
1 cup light cream

Melt butter in saucepan; blend in flour and salt. Gradually add water and cook, stirring constantly, until mixture thickens and comes to a boil. Add onion and green beans and cook, covered, until beans are tender, about 25 minutes. Add tuna and cream; heat to serving temperature.

YIELD: 4 servings.

CATALINA TUNA CASSEROLE

¼ cup butter or margarine
2 tablespoons flour
1 cup milk
1 egg yolk, well beaten

1 teaspoon lemon juice
1 can (6½ or 7 ounces) tuna, drained and flaked
½ cup sliced ripe olives
1 package (10 ounces) frozen lima beans, cooked
½ teaspoon salt
½ teaspoon paprika

Melt butter in saucepan; blend in flour. Gradually add milk and cook, stirring constantly, until mixture thickens and comes to a boil. Add a little of hot mixture to egg yolk; mix well. Add to remaining hot mixture. Add remaining ingredients; mix lightly but thoroughly. Turn into a greased 1-quart casserole; cover. Bake in a 375° F. oven 15 minutes.

YIELD: *4 servings.*

TUNA-RICE CURRY

6 tablespoons butter or margarine, divided
¼ cup flour
½ teaspoon curry powder
2 cups milk
1 beef bouillon cube
1 cup shredded Cheddar cheese
1 can (9¼ ounces) tuna, drained and flaked
3 tablespoons chopped parsley
3 cups hot cooked rice

Melt 3 tablespoons butter in saucepan; blend in flour and curry powder. Gradually add milk and bouillon cube and cook, stirring constantly, until mixture thickens and comes to a boil. Add Cheddar cheese and tuna; continue cooking until cheese has melted. Add remaining butter and parsley to hot rice; toss lightly until well mixed. Spoon rice in a ring around edge of serving platter; fill center with hot tuna mixture. Garnish with parsley, if desired.

YIELD: *4 servings.*

TUNA-CRANBERRY TOSSED SALAD

2 cups cranberries
1 cup sugar
⅓ cup hot water
2 cans (6½ or 7 ounces each) tuna
⅓ cup vinegar
2 teaspoons celery seed
½ teaspoon salt
Salad oil
1½ cups orange chunks
3 cups torn in pieces spinach
3 cups torn in pieces lettuce

Combine cranberries, sugar, and water in saucepan; cook over high heat until mixture boils. Cool; drain cranberry mixture and reserve ⅓ cup liquid. Chill cranberries. Drain tuna and reserve oil; break tuna into pieces. Combine cranberry liquid, vinegar, celery seed, and salt. Add enough salad oil to tuna oil to make ⅔ cup. Gradually add oil mixture to vinegar mixture, beating constantly. Combine tuna, cranberries, orange chunks, spinach, and lettuce; add cranberry salad dressing and toss lightly.

YIELD   6 servings.

TUNA FLORENTINE

2 cans (6½ or 7 ounces each) tuna
¼ cup flour
2 cups milk
1 teaspoon salt
¼ teaspoon pepper
3 tablespoons lemon juice

¼ cup butter or margarine
Dash cayenne
3 egg yolks, well beaten
1 package (10 ounces) frozen chopped spinach, cooked
    and drained
½ cup buttered bread crumbs
Paprika

Drain tuna; reserve ¼ cup oil. Heat tuna oil in saucepan over low heat; blend in flour. Gradually add milk and cook, stirring constantly, until mixture thickens and comes to a boil. Add salt and pepper. Stir in lemon juice, butter, and cayenne. Add a little of hot mixture to egg yolks. Add egg mixture to remaining hot mixture and mix well. Cook over low heat until thickened, stirring constantly. Arrange spinach in a greased 2-quart casserole. Combine tuna and sauce and spoon over spinach. Sprinkle with crumbs and dust with paprika. Bake in 375° F. oven 25 to 30 minutes or until crumbs are golden brown.

YIELD: *6 servings.*

TUNA BALLS WITH SPAGHETTI

2 cans (6½ or 7 ounces each) tuna
2 tablespoons chopped onion
1 can (1 pound, 4 ounces) tomatoes
1 can (6 ounces) tomato paste
1 teaspoon dried leaf oregano
1 teaspoon salt
⅛ teaspoon pepper
2 eggs
¾ cup fine dry bread crumbs, divided
¼ teaspoon dried leaf marjoram
2 tablespoons butter or margarine
8 ounces spaghetti

Drain tuna and reserve 2 tablespoons oil. Heat tuna oil in saucepan over low heat; add onion and cook until tender. Add tomatoes, tomato paste, oregano, salt, and pepper; mix thoroughly. Cover and cook over low heat 20 minutes, stirring occasionally. Combine tuna, eggs, ½ cup crumbs and marjoram; mix well. Shape tuna mixture into 8 balls. Roll in remaining crumbs. Melt butter in skillet; add tuna balls. Cook over medium heat until lightly browned. Add to tomato sauce and cook 5 minutes. Meanwhile, cook spaghetti in boiling salted water according to package directions. Drain. Place on serving platter; top with tuna mixture.

YIELD: *4 servings.*

DEEP-DISH TUNA PIE

2 cans (6½ or 7 ounces each) tuna
3 tablespoons flour
½ teaspoon salt
⅛ teaspoon pepper
2 cups milk
6 medium carrots, sliced and cooked
12 small onions, cooked
1 cup cooked peas
1 recipe pie pastry

Drain tuna and reserve 3 tablespoons oil. Heat tuna oil in saucepan; blend in flour, salt, and pepper. Gradually add milk and cook, stirring constantly, until mixture thickens and comes to a boil. Add tuna and vegetables to sauce; mix lightly. Divide pastry into 2 portions. Roll out each portion to ⅛-inch thickness on lightly floured surface. Line a 1-quart casserole with half of pastry. Fill with tuna-vegetable mixture. Cover with remaining pastry and seal edges. Cut slashes in top crust. Bake in a 425° F. oven 30 minutes or until crust is golden brown.

YIELD: *6 servings.*

TUNA AU GRATIN

3 tablespoons butter or margarine
⅓ cup finely chopped green pepper
3 tablespoons finely chopped onion
2 tablespoons flour
1 cup milk
1 can (6½ or 7 ounces) tuna, drained and flaked
½ teaspoon salt
⅛ teaspoon pepper
½ teaspoon Worcestershire sauce
1½ tablespoons chopped canned pimiento

Melt butter in saucepan over low heat. Add green pepper and onion and cook until tender. Blend in flour. Gradually add milk and cook, stirring constantly, until mixture thickens and comes to a boil. Add tuna, salt, pepper, Worcestershire sauce, and pimiento to sauce; mix well. Pour into 4 greased individual casseroles. If desired, sprinkle grated cheese over each casserole. Bake in 375° F. oven 15 minutes.

YIELD: *4 servings.*

TUNA-CRANBERRY RAGOUT

2 tablespoons butter or margarine
2 tablespoons flour
1 chicken bouillon cube
1½ cups boiling water
2 cans (6½ or 7 ounces each) tuna, drained and flaked
½ teaspoon Worcestershire sauce
Dash nutmeg
½ cup canned whole cranberry sauce
1 tablespoon dry sherry
6 toast cups, optional

Melt butter in saucepan over low heat; blend in flour. Dissolve bouillon cube in water. Gradually add bouillon to flour mixture; cook, stirring constantly, until mixture thickens and comes to a boil. Add tuna, Worcestershire sauce, and nutmeg; heat. Add cranberry sauce and sherry; mix well. Heat to serving temperature. Serve in toast cups, if desired.

YIELD: *6 servings.*

TUNA-ARTICHOKE CASSEROLE

1 jar (8 ounces) artichoke hearts, drained
1 can (6½ or 7 ounces) tuna, drained
1 can (3 ounces) sliced mushrooms, drained
2 tablespoons butter or margarine
2 tablespoons flour
1½ cups milk
½ teaspoon salt
Dash pepper
1 tablespoon Worcestershire sauce
¼ cup grated Parmesan cheese

Arrange artichokes in a greased 1-quart casserole. Break tuna into large pieces and place over artichokes. Top with mushrooms. Melt butter in saucepan; blend in flour. Gradually add milk and cook, stirring constantly, until mixture thickens and comes to a boil. Add salt, pepper, and Worcestershire sauce. Pour sauce over ingredients in casserole; sprinkle with cheese. Bake in 375° F. oven 20 minutes.

YIELD: *4 to 6 servings.*

TUNA AND CHEESE BEANBURGERS

5 tablespoons butter or margarine, divided
1 medium onion, finely chopped

1 can (1 pound) kidney beans, drained
2 cups soft bread crumbs
1 egg, well beaten
½ cup chopped sweet gherkins
1 can (6½ or 7 ounces) tuna, drained and flaked
Salt
Pepper
Flour
6 slices process American cheese

Melt 1 tablespoon butter in saucepan over low heat; add onion and cook until tender. Mash kidney beans; add onion, bread crumbs, egg, gherkins, tuna, salt, and pepper; mix well. Shape tuna mixture into 6 patties and dredge with flour. Melt remaining butter in skillet. Add patties and cook on both sides until browned. Place 1 slice cheese over each patty; cover and cook until cheese is melted.

YIELD: *6 servings.*

BLUE CHEESE AND TUNA CASSEROLE

2 cans (6½ or 7 ounces each) tuna
2 tablespoons flour
2 cups milk
1 cup crumbled blue cheese (about 5 ounces)
3½ cups cooked rice
1 can (1 pound) tomatoes
¼ cup chopped parsley

Drain tuna and reserve 2 tablespoons oil; break tuna into pieces. Heat tuna oil in saucepan over low heat; blend in flour. Gradually add milk and cook over low heat, stirring constantly, until mixture thickens and comes to a boil. Add cheese and stir until cheese is melted. Arrange alternate layers of rice, tomatoes, cheese sauce, and tuna in a greased 1½-quart casserole. Bake in 350° F. oven 40 minutes. Sprinkle with parsley.

YIELD: *6 servings.*

SCALLOPED TUNA AND POTATO CASSEROLE

4 medium potatoes, pared and thinly sliced
1 can (4 ounces) sliced mushrooms, drained
1 can (6½ or 7 ounces) tuna, drained and flaked
2 tablespoons finely chopped pimiento
½ cup shredded Cheddar cheese
1 teaspoon salt
¼ teaspoon pepper
1 cup milk
2 tablespoons melted butter or margarine
½ cup fine dry bread crumbs
Paprika

Alternate layers of potatoes, mushrooms, tuna, pimiento, and cheese in a greased 2-quart casserole. Sprinkle with salt and pepper. Pour milk over tuna mixture. Combine butter and bread crumbs; sprinkle over top. Dust with paprika. Bake in 375° F. oven 1 hour or until potatoes are tender.

YIELD: *4 servings.*

TUNA-BROCCOLI CASSEROLE

1 can (6½ or 7 ounces) tuna
2 tablespoons flour
½ teaspoon salt
⅛ teaspoon pepper
1 cup milk

1 package (10 ounces) frozen broccoli, cooked
3 tablespoons grated Parmesan cheese

Drain tuna and reserve 2 tablespoons oil. Heat tuna oil in saucepan over low heat; blend in flour, salt, and pepper. Gradually add milk and cook, stirring constantly, until mixture thickens and comes to a boil. Arrange broccoli and tuna in greased 1-quart casserole. Pour sauce over top. Sprinkle with cheese. Bake in 350° F. oven 15 minutes.

YIELD: *4 servings.*

BAKED TUNA IN WINE AND EGG SAUCE

2 cans (6½ or 7 ounces each) tuna
1 package (10 ounces) frozen peas, cooked
3 tablespoons flour
1 cup milk
½ cup dry white wine
1 tablespoon capers
2 hard-cooked eggs, chopped
¼ teaspoon dried leaf basil
Salt
Pepper

Drain tuna and reserve 3 tablespoons oil. Break tuna into large pieces. Turn tuna and peas into a greased 1½-quart casserole. Heat tuna oil in saucepan over low heat; blend in flour. Gradually add milk and cook, stirring constantly, until mixture thickens and comes to a boil. Add wine with remaining ingredients. Pour sauce over ingredients in casserole. Bake in 350° F. oven 30 minutes.

YIELD: *4 to 6 servings.*

SAUCY TUNA COOK-IN

6 tablespoons butter or margarine
6 tablespoons flour
3 cups milk or equal amounts of milk and cream
¼ cup chopped onion
3 tablespoons chopped pimiento
1⅓ cups shredded Gruyère cheese
1 cup grated Parmesan cheese
½ teaspoon Ac'cent
1 can (4 ounces) mushrooms, drained
2 cans (6½ or 7 ounces each) tuna, drained and flaked

Melt butter in saucepan; blend in flour. Gradually add milk and cook, stirring constantly, until mixture thickens and comes to a boil. Add onion, pimiento, Gruyère and Parmesan cheeses, and Ac'cent. Stir until cheeses are melted. Add mushrooms and tuna. Serve hot on toasted rusks or English muffins.

YIELD: *6 servings.*

CHOW MEIN LOAF

3 cups medium white sauce, divided
½ teaspoon Worcestershire sauce
2 eggs, separated
1 can (6½ or 7 ounces) tuna, drained and flaked
⅓ cup peanut halves
3 cups chow mein noodles, divided
¼ cup chopped pimiento
2 tablespoons finely chopped parsley

Combine 1¼ cups of the white sauce with Worcestershire sauce, 2 well-beaten egg yolks, tuna, peanuts, and 2 cups of the chow mein noodles. Beat egg whites until stiff, but not dry; fold into tuna mixture and turn into a greased 9×5×3-inch loaf pan. Bake in 350° F. oven 30 minutes or until golden-brown crust is formed. Unmold on hot platter and surround with remaining crisp noodles. Serve with remaining 1¾ cups white sauce to which ¼ cup chopped pimiento and 2 table-spoons finely chopped parsley have been added.

YIELD: *6 servings.*

TUNA BEAN SUPPER DISH

> *2 tablespoons butter or margarine*
> *¼ cup minced onion*
> *1 can (10½ ounces) condensed cream of celery soup*
> *½ cup milk*
> *1 can (6½ or 7 ounces) tuna, drained and flaked*
> *2 hard-cooked eggs, chopped*
> *2 tablespoons chopped pimiento*
> *1 pound green beans, cooked and drained*

Melt butter in saucepan; add onion and cook until tender. Blend in soup, milk, tuna, eggs, and pimiento. Heat to serving temperature. Arrange hot beans around edge of serving dish; spoon creamed mixture in the center.

YIELD: *6 servings.*

TUNA CHILI PIE WITH CEREAL CRUST

FILLING:

> 2 tablespoons butter or margarine
> 1 cup coarsely chopped onion
> 1 clove garlic, minced
> ¾ cup chopped celery
> 1 can (1 pound, 4 ounces) tomatoes
> 1 can (8 ounces) tomato sauce
> 1 can (12 ounces) whole-kernel corn, drained
> 2 cans (6½ or 7 ounces each) tuna, drained and flaked
> 1 teaspoon salt
> ¼ teaspoon pepper
> 2 to 3 teaspoons chili powder

Melt butter in a skillet. Add onion, garlic, and celery; cook 5 minutes until onion is tender. Add tomatoes, tomato sauce, corn, tuna, salt, pepper, and chili powder. Cover and cook 15 minutes. Set aside.

CRUST:

> 1½ cups sifted all-purpose flour
> 2 teaspoons baking powder
> 1½ teaspoons salt
> 2 teaspoons sugar
> 1¾ cups whole wheat cereal, uncooked, or 1¾ cups
>   farina, plain or malt-flavored, uncooked
> 1 cup milk
> 1 egg, beaten
> ⅔ cup melted shortening

Sift flour, baking powder, salt, and sugar into mixing bowl. Stir in uncooked cereal. Combine milk, egg, and shortening; add to dry ingredients, stirring just until dry ingredients are moistened. Let stand 5 minutes. Save ⅔ cup of mixture for top. Spread remaining crust evenly over bottom and sides of greased 11¾ × 7½ × 1¾-inch baking dish, bringing crust up onto edge of dish to form a high rim. Pour hot filling into crust and top with spoonfuls of crust mixture. Bake in a 350° F. oven until crust is done and mixture is hot and bubbly, 35 to 40 minutes.

YIELD: *8 servings.*

SEA-SPRAY SALAD

2 tablespoons unflavored gelatin
1 cup cold water
1 package (3 ounces) cream cheese, crumbled
2 teaspoons prepared mustard
1 teaspoon salt
¼ teaspoon paprika
3 tablespoons lemon juice
¾ cup chopped celery
¼ cup chopped green pepper
¼ cup finely chopped onion
2 cans (6½ or 7 ounces each) tuna, drained and flaked
Salad greens

Sprinkle gelatin on cold water to soften. Place over low heat and stir until gelatin is dissolved. Combine gelatin mixture, cream cheese, mustard, salt, paprika, and lemon juice; beat until blended. Chill until mixture mounds slightly when dropped from a spoon. Fold in remaining ingredients except salad greens. Turn into 1-quart mold and chill until firm. Unmold and surround with crisp salad greens.

YIELD: *6 servings.*

MOLDED TUNA-LIME SALAD

1 package (3 ounces) lime-flavored gelatin
1 cup hot water
1 package (3 ounces) cream cheese, broken into chunks
1 cup cold water
½ cup drained canned crushed pineapple
1 can (6½ or 7 ounces) tuna, drained and flaked

Dissolve gelatin in hot water. Add cream cheese and stir until cheese is partially melted. Add cold water and mix well; chill until slightly thickened. Fold in remaining ingredients. Turn into 1-quart mold and chill until firm. Unmold to serve.

YIELD:　*4 to 6 servings.*

TUNA-AU-GRATIN PIE

¼ cup milk
1 can (10½ ounces) mushroom soup
2 tablespoons flour
⅓ cup chopped onion
1 package (10 ounces) frozen peas, thawed and drained
2 cans (6½ or 7 ounces each) tuna, drained and flaked
2 tablespoons chopped pimiento
1 (9-inch) baked pastry shell
1 cup shredded Cheddar cheese

Combine milk, soup, flour, and onion in a saucepan. Cook and stir until mixture comes to a boil and is thickened. Remove from heat; stir in peas, tuna, and pimiento. Turn into baked pastry shell. Top with cheese. Bake in a 425° F. oven 12 to 15 minutes or until cheese melts.

YIELD:　*6 to 8 servings.*

PASTA
AND
RICE

CASSEROLE CAPRI

¼ cup butter or margarine
1 cup sliced fresh mushrooms
1 cup uncooked rice
2 cups water
1 tablespoon minced onion
½ teaspoon fines herbes
3 tomatoes
2 cans (6½ or 7 ounces each) tuna, drained and flaked
1 cup shredded, sharp Cheddar cheese
½ cup buttered crumbs

Melt butter in a small skillet. Add mushrooms and cook 5 minutes. Turn into a 2-quart casserole. Add rice to skillet and cook until lightly browned. Add to casserole with water, onion, and fines herbes. Chop 2 tomatoes coarsely; add to casserole with tuna. Cover and bake in 375° F. oven 45 minutes. Remove cover; stir in grated cheese. Slice remaining tomato into wedges; arrange over casserole. Top with buttered crumbs. Place under broiler 2 to 3 minutes until top is lightly browned. Serve at once.

YIELD: *6 servings.*

SALMON RICE WITH VEGETABLE KABOBS

1 can (1 pound) salmon
½ cup chopped onion
2 tablespoons butter or margarine, melted
⅔ cup water
1 can (10½ ounces) condensed consommé
1 cup uncooked rice
3 tomatoes
3 green peppers
18 fresh mushrooms
½ cup butter or margarine, melted

Drain salmon. Break salmon into large pieces. Cook onion in butter in saucepan until tender. Add water and consommé; bring to a boil. Place rice, salmon, and consommé mixture in a well-greased, 2-quart casserole. Stir. Bake, covered, in a 350° F. oven 35 minutes or until rice is tender. While rice is baking, cut tomatoes and green peppers into sixths. Remove stems from mushrooms. Alternate tomatoes, green peppers, and mushrooms on 6 skewers, 7 inches long. Place on a greased broiler pan. Brush kabobs with butter. Broil about 3 inches from heat for 3 minutes. Turn carefully; brush other side with butter and broil 3 minutes longer. Serve salmon-rice mixture on a platter with kabobs on top.

YIELD: *6 servings.*

RISOTTO AL VERDE
(Rice with Vegetables)

½ cup salad oil
1 pound fresh spinach, chopped
¼ pound green beans, chopped
1 cup coarsely grated carrots

1 medium onion, chopped
1 clove garlic, chopped
½ teaspoon dried leaf thyme
2 teaspoons salt
1 quart water
2 cups precooked rice
Grated Parmesan cheese

Pour oil into saucepan and place over moderate heat. Add spinach, beans, carrots, onion, garlic, thyme, and salt. Cook until onion is slightly browned. Add water and continue cooking for about 10 minutes. Then add rice cooked according to package directions. Heat. Sprinkle with Parmesan cheese.

YIELD: *6 servings.*

SPINACH-RICE FRITTATA

2 tablespoons butter or margarine
½ cup finely chopped onion
1½ cups drained, cooked, chopped spinach
1 clove garlic, crushed
3 cups cooked rice
½ cup grated Parmesan cheese
4 eggs, slightly beaten
½ cup milk
2 teaspoons salt
¼ teaspoon pepper
1 cup shredded mozzarella cheese

Melt butter in saucepan. Add onion and cook until tender. Add spinach, garlic, rice, and Parmesan cheese; mix well. Combine eggs, milk, and seasonings. Stir into rice mixture. Turn into a well-buttered shallow 2-quart casserole. Top with cheese. Bake in a 350° F. oven 30 minutes or until cheese is melted.

YIELD: *6 servings.*

GOLDEN RICE SALAD

¼ cup salad oil
2 tablespoons vinegar
2 tablespoons prepared mustard
1½ teaspoons salt
⅛ teaspoon pepper
4½ cups hot cooked rice
1 cup cut in large pieces ripe olives
2 hard-cooked eggs, diced
1½ cups sliced celery
¼ cup chopped dill pickles
¼ cup cut-up pimiento
1 small onion, minced
½ cup mayonnaise
Salad greens

Blend together salad oil, vinegar, mustard, salt, and pepper;
pour over hot rice; toss and set aside to cool. Add remaining
ingredients except salad greens; toss. Chill thoroughly. Serve
on salad greens.

YIELD: 6 servings.

DEVILED RICE

2 tablespoons butter or margarine
½ cup chopped onion
½ cup chopped green pepper
⅓ cup sour cream
⅓ cup currant jelly
¼ cup prepared mustard
2 tablespoons chopped pimiento
1 teaspoon Worcestershire sauce
3 cups hot cooked rice

Melt butter in saucepan; add onion and green pepper and
cook until tender. Add sour cream, currant jelly, mustard,

pimiento, and Worcestershire sauce. Mix well and heat, stirring occasionally. Combine with hot rice.

YIELD: *5 servings.*

SPANISH RICE AU GRATIN

½ cup uncooked rice
1 cup water
½ teaspoon salt
½ cup chopped onion
⅓ cup chopped green pepper
½ cup chopped celery
1½ tablespoons butter or margarine
1 cup canned tomatoes
½ teaspoon Ac'cent
1 teaspoon sugar
1 teaspoon chili powder
½ teaspoon Worcestershire sauce
1 cup shredded Cheddar cheese

Combine rice, water, and salt. Bring to a boil. Stir; cover and reduce heat. Simmer for 14 minutes. Meanwhile, cook onion, green pepper, and celery in butter. Add tomatoes, Ac'cent, sugar, chili powder, and Worcestershire sauce. Add cooked rice and simmer until thick. Pour into a buttered casserole and top with cheese. Place under broiler until cheese is melted.

YIELD: *6 servings.*

MACARONI WITH BEANS

1 pound elbow macaroni
3 tablespoons butter
¼ cup chopped onion
¼ cup chopped green pepper
2 cans (8 ounces each) tomato sauce with mushrooms
1 can (1 pound) red kidney beans, drained
1 cup shredded American cheese

Cook macaroni in boiling salted water according to package directions. Melt butter in saucepan. Add onion and green pepper and cook until onion is tender. Add tomato sauce. Add macaroni and beans and allow to heat thoroughly. Sprinkle with cheese before serving.

YIELD: *6 servings.*

SUPER MACARONI AND CHEESE

> *2 cups cooked elbow macaroni*
> *1 tablespoon butter or margarine*
> *1 can (10¾ ounces) condensed cream of mushroom*
>   *soup*
> *⅓ cup water*
> *1 cup shredded Cheddar cheese, divided*
> *1 tablespoon finely minced onion*

Blend hot cooked macaroni with butter in a 1½-quart casserole. Blend together soup and water. Add to macaroni with ¾ cup cheese, and onion. Mix well. Sprinkle remaining cheese on top. Bake in a 350° F. oven about 30 minutes or until heated through.

YIELD: *4 servings.*

Tomato Macaroni: Use ingredients and directions as above, but substitute 1 can (10¾ ounces) condensed tomato soup for the cream of mushroom soup.

MACARONI CREOLE LOAF

> *2 cups cooked elbow macaroni*
> *1 cup soft bread crumbs*
> *2 eggs*

½ *teaspoon salt*
2 *tablespoons chopped green pepper*
⅔ *cup shredded American cheese*
1¼ *cups canned tomatoes*
¼ *cup salad oil*
1½ *tablespoons prepared mustard*
Dash celery salt
Dash pepper

Combine ingredients. Turn into 1½-quart casserole. Bake in a 350° F. oven 35 minutes.

YIELD: *4 servings.*

FETTUCINE WITH SWEET-SOUR TUNA SAUCE

1 *teaspoon dried leaf basil*
½ *cup wine vinegar*
1 *medium onion, sliced*
2 *tablespoons olive oil*
1 *tablespoon flour*
2 *cans (6½ or 7 ounces each) tuna, drained and flaked*
¼ *cup sliced pitted black olives*
2 *teaspoons sugar*
½ *teaspoon salt*
¼ *teaspoon pepper*
8 *ounces medium noodles*
Chopped parsley
Shelled pine nuts or chopped peanuts, optional

Soak basil in wine vinegar about ½ hour to freshen it. Cook onion in olive oil in saucepan until tender, but not brown; blend in flour. Add tuna, olives, sugar, salt, pepper, and basil-vinegar mixture. Heat through. Meanwhile, cook noodles in boiling salted water according to package directions. Drain and arrange on heated platter. Pour tuna sauce over noodles. Garnish with parsley and pine nuts or peanuts.

YIELD:　*4 to 6 servings.*

RING OF PLENTY

> *4 cups cooked macaroni*
> *2 cups hot milk*
> *¼ cup butter*
> *2 cups shredded American cheese*
> *2 cups soft bread crumbs*
> *2 eggs, well beaten*
> *2 tablespoons minced parsley*
> *2 tablespoons minced onion*
> *2 tablespoons chopped pimiento*
> *2 teaspoons salt*
> *¼ teaspoon pepper*
> *1 pouch (6½ ounces) lobster or shrimp Newburg,*
> *　　cooked according to package directions*

Combine all ingredients except lobster. Turn into a well-greased 10-inch ring mold set in a pan of water. Bake in 350° F. oven 30 to 35 minutes or until set. Unmold on hot platter; fill center with lobster or shrimp Newburg.

YIELD:　*6 to 8 servings.*

SALMON PASTA

> *1 can (8 ounces) salmon, drained*
> *1 pound ricotta cheese*
> *12 large pasta shells*
> *3 tablespoons butter or margarine*
> *3 tablespoons flour*
> *½ teaspoon salt*

⅛ *teaspoon pepper*
⅛ *teaspoon nutmeg*
1 cup milk
1 cup cooked, chopped spinach
½ *cup grated Parmesan cheese*

Combine salmon and cheese; mix well. Cook pasta shells in boiling salted water according to package directions. Drain. Melt butter in saucepan; blend in flour and seasonings. Add milk gradually and cook until thick and smooth, stirring constantly. Add spinach and blend thoroughly. Pour sauce into a well-greased 8×8×2-inch baking dish. Fill pasta shells with salmon mixture and arrange over spinach. Sprinkle with cheese. Bake in 350° F. oven 30 minutes.

YIELD: *6 servings.*

QUICK COTTAGE CHEESE LASAGNE

8 ounces lasagne
2 cans (8 ounces each) tomato sauce
2 cups creamed cottage cheese
½ *pound Cheddar cheese, sliced*
1 teaspoon salt
¼ *teaspoon Worcestershire sauce*
¼ *cup finely chopped onion*
½ *pound Cheddar cheese, sliced*
½ *cup buttered bread crumbs*
¼ *cup grated Parmesan cheese*

Cook lasagne in boiling salted water according to package directions. Drain. Combine tomato sauce, cottage cheese, basil, salt, Worcestershire sauce, and onion. Arrange alternate layers of lasagne, Cheddar cheese, and sauce mixture in a 2½-quart casserole. Top with buttered bread crumbs mixed with Parmesan cheese. Bake in 350° F. oven 30 to 35 minutes.

YIELD: *6 servings.*

MACARONI-SALMON SALAD

2 cups cooked shell macaroni
1 cup diced, peeled cucumber
1 can (8 ounces) salmon, drained and flaked
1 tablespoon minced onion
1 tablespoon minced parsley
¾ cup mayonnaise
½ teaspoon salt
¼ teaspoon pepper
Salad greens

Combine all ingredients except salad greens. Mix well and chill. Place salad greens on serving platter. Spoon macaroni mixture in center.

YIELD: 4 servings.

SPAGHETTI WITH RICOTTA

1 pound spaghetti
½ pound butter, melted
1 pound ricotta cheese
1 cup grated Parmesan or Romano cheese
Salt
Pepper
Chopped parsley, optional

Cook spaghetti in boiling salted water according to package directions. Drain; return to saucepan. Add melted butter. Mix ricotta until smooth. Add to spaghetti with remaining ingredients except parsley; toss lightly. If desired, sprinkle with chopped parsley.

YIELD: 6 to 8 servings.

BAKED SALMON WITH NOODLES

1 can (1 pound) salmon
3 cups cooked noodles
¼ cup minced onion
2 tablespoons chopped parsley
2 tablespoons chopped pickle
¾ teaspoon salt
⅛ teaspoon pepper
⅓ cup milk
½ cup buttered bread crumbs

Coarsely flake salmon. Combine salmon and salmon liquid with remaining ingredients except crumbs. Toss lightly. Turn into greased 1½-quart baking dish; sprinkle with bread crumbs. Bake in 375° F. oven 30 minutes or until heated through.

YIELD: *4 servings.*

SALMON SPAGHETTI BAKE

1 can (3 or 4 ounces) sliced mushrooms, drained
2 tablespoons minced onion
3 tablespoons butter or margarine, divided
2 tablespoons flour
½ teaspoon salt
Dash pepper
1 can (1 pound) salmon; drain and reserve liquid
Milk
3 cups cooked spaghetti
⅓ cup grated Parmesan cheese
½ cup buttered cracker crumbs

Cook mushrooms and onion in 1 tablespoon butter 5 minutes. Melt remaining 2 tablespoons butter in medium saucepan;

blend in flour and seasonings. Add liquid drained from salmon plus enough milk to make 1½ cups. Cook, stirring constantly, until mixture thickens and comes to a boil. Fold in flaked salmon, cooked spaghetti, cheese, mushrooms and onions. Turn into a greased 1½-quart baking dish; sprinkle with cracker crumbs. Bake in 400° F. oven 20 minutes or until heated through.

YIELD: *4 servings.*

QUICK SALMON-MACARONI SUPPER

1 can (8 ounces) salmon, drained and flaked
2 cans (about 1 pound each) macaroni and cheese
½ cup finely chopped celery
1 teaspoon grated onion
½ teaspoon dry mustard
2 tablespoons milk
Garlic croutons

Combine salmon, macaroni and cheese, celery, onion, mustard, and milk. Turn into a greased 1½-quart baking dish; sprinkle with croutons. Bake in 350° F. oven 30 to 35 minutes, or until heated through.

YIELD: *4 servings.*

SALMON TETRAZZINI

1 can (1 pound) salmon; drain and reserve liquid
2 tablespoons butter or margarine
2 tablespoons flour
½ teaspoon salt
Dash pepper
Dash nutmeg

Milk
1 tablespoon dry sherry
2 cups cooked spaghetti
1 can (3 or 4 ounces) sliced mushrooms, drained
2 tablespoons grated Parmesan cheese
2 tablespoons dry bread crumbs

Break salmon into large pieces. Melt butter in saucepan; blend in flour and seasonings. Gradually add salmon liquid and milk to make 2 cups and cook, stirring constantly, until mixture thickens and comes to a boil. Add sherry. Mix half of the sauce with spaghetti and mushrooms. Turn into a well-greased, 2-quart casserole. Combine remaining sauce with salmon. Place in center of spaghetti. Combine cheese and crumbs; sprinkle over top of salmon mixture. Bake in 350° F. oven 25 to 30 minutes.

YIELD: *6 servings.*

MACARONI SUPPER CASSEROLE

4 cups cooked elbow macaroni
½ cup mayonnaise
¼ cup diced green pepper
¼ cup chopped pimiento
1 small onion, chopped
½ teaspoon salt
1 can (10¾ ounces) cream of mushroom soup
½ cup milk
1 cup shredded American cheese, divided

Combine all ingredients and ½ cup of the cheese. Turn into a 1½-quart baking dish. Sprinkle with remaining ½ cup cheese. Bake in a 400° F. oven 20 minutes.

YIELD: *6 servings.*

MACARONI AND CHEESE

¼ cup chopped onion
1 tablespoon butter or margarine
1 can (11 ounces) condensed Cheddar cheese soup
½ cup milk
3 cups cooked macaroni

Cook onion in butter in saucepan until tender but not brown. Blend in soup; gradually add milk. Heat; stir often. Mix in macaroni. Heat to serving temperature, stirring occasionally.

YIELD: *4 servings.*

SHRIMP AND MACARONI TOSS

1 can (10¾ ounces) condensed cream of chicken soup
¼ cup chopped celery
¼ cup chopped onion
2 tablespoons chopped green pepper
½ teaspoon prepared mustard
⅛ teaspoon Tabasco
2 cups cooked shell macaroni
1 cup diced cooked shrimp
Salad greens
Tomato wedges

Combine soup, celery, onion, green pepper, mustard, and Tabasco. Add macaroni and shrimp. Chill. Serve on salad greens with tomato wedges.

YIELD: *4 servings.*

OVEN MACARONI

¼ cup chopped onion
1 tablespoon butter or margarine
1 can (11 ounces) condensed Cheddar cheese soup
½ cup milk
2 cups cooked macaroni
2 tablespoons buttered bread crumbs

Cook onion in butter in saucepan until tender but not brown.
Blend in soup; gradually stir in milk. Combine sauce and
cooked macaroni in a buttered 1-quart casserole. Sprinkle
crumbs on top. Bake in a 375° F. oven about 30 minutes or until heated through.

YIELD: *4 servings.*

MACARONI, CHEESE, AND EGG CASSEROLE

1 cup broken macaroni
1½ cups water
½ cup instant nonfat dry milk
2 tablespoons flour
½ teaspoon salt
1½ tablespoons butter or margarine
1½ cups shredded American cheese
4 hard-cooked eggs, sliced
¼ cup buttered bread crumbs

Cook macaroni in boiling salted water according to package
directions. Drain. Put water into a saucepan; add nonfat dry
milk, flour, and salt. Stir until smooth. Add butter and cook
over low heat, stirring constantly, until mixture thickens and

comes to a boil. Remove from heat; add cheese and stir until melted. Place macaroni in a buttered baking dish. Cover with sliced eggs and top with cheese sauce. Sprinkle crumbs over top. Bake in 350° F. oven 30 minutes.

YIELD: *4 servings.*

COTTAGE CHEESE MANICOTTI

12 manicotti shells
3 cups creamed cottage cheese
2 tablespoons minced onion
1 teaspoon salt
½ teaspoon paprika
1 package (10 ounces) frozen chopped spinach, thawed
*   and moisture pressed out*
2 eggs, well beaten
¾ cup grated Parmesan cheese, divided
½ cup cracker crumbs
¼ cup butter or margarine
¼ cup flour
1 cup milk
1 cup sour cream
Salt
Pepper
⅓ cup slivered blanched almonds

Cook manicotti shells in boiling salted water for 2 minutes. Drain and put in cold water. Combine cottage cheese, onion, salt, paprika, spinach, eggs, ½ cup of the Parmesan cheese, and cracker crumbs; mix well. Drain manicotti and use cheese mixture to fill shells. Put filled shells side by side in a greased shallow pan. Melt butter in saucepan; blend in flour. Gradually add milk and sour cream. Cook over low heat, stirring constantly, until mixture thickens and comes to a boil. Add remaining ¼ cup Parmesan cheese and salt and pepper to taste. Spoon sauce over manicotti; sprinkle with slivered al-

monds. Bake in 350° F. oven 35 to 40 minutes or until sauce is
golden brown and bubbly.

Yield: *6 servings.*

LASAGNA

Sauce:

> 2 tablespoons butter or margarine
> 1 clove garlic, finely chopped
> ½ cup chopped onion
> 2 cans (8 ounces each) tomato sauce
> 1 can (1 pound) tomatoes
> 1 tablespoon brown sugar
> 1½ teaspoons dried leaf basil
> 1 teaspoon dried leaf oregano
> 1 teaspoon salt
> 1 bay leaf

Melt butter in large saucepan. Add garlic and onion; cook until
onion is tender, but not brown. Add remaining ingredients
and simmer slowly 30 minutes, stirring occasionally. Remove
bay leaf. (Sauce can be cooked in advance and refrigerated
until ready to be used.)

Casserole:

> ½ pound lasagna
> 1 pint creamed cottage cheese
> 1 egg, slightly beaten
> ¼ cup chopped parsley
> 1 teaspoon salt
> ¼ teaspoon pepper
> ½ cup grated Parmesan cheese
> 10 hard-cooked eggs, sliced
> 12 ounces mozzarella cheese, thinly sliced
> Parsley

Cook lasagna noodles in boiling salted water according to package directions. Drain. Arrange on waxed paper to prevent noodles from sticking together. Combine cottage cheese, egg, parsley, salt, pepper and Parmesan cheese. Spread ⅓ of sauce in shallow 11½ ×7½ ×1½ -inch baking dish. Arrange in layers half of the lasagna, half of the cottage cheese mixture, half of the eggs (reserve center slices for garnish), and half of the mozzarella. Repeat sauce and layers, ending with sauce. Bake in 350° F. oven 35 to 40 minutes. Garnish with egg slices and parsley. Let stand 5 minutes before serving.

YIELD: *8 to 10 servings.*

CREAMED SALMON ON NOODLE MOLD

NOODLE MOLD:

> *3 tablespoons fine dry bread crumbs*
> *2 eggs*
> *1 cup milk*
> *¾ teaspoon salt*
> *⅛ teaspoon pepper*
> *2 tablespoons catchup*
> *½ cup grated American cheese*
> *¼ teaspoon Worcestershire sauce*
> *8 ounces medium noodles, cooked*

Grease an 8-inch square pan with oil; sprinkle with bread crumbs. Beat eggs; add remaining ingredients. Turn into prepared pan; bake in pan of hot water in 325° F. oven about 40 minutes. Serve with creamed salmon.

CREAMED SALMON:

> *1 can (1 pound) salmon*
> *¼ cup salad oil*

> ½ *cup chopped green pepper*
> 1 *cup sliced fresh or canned mushrooms, drained*
> ¼ *cup flour*
> 1 *teaspoon salt*
> 1 *cup milk*
> 2 *egg yolks*
> 1 *cup sour cream*

Drain salmon; reserve liquid. Heat oil in saucepan. Sauté green pepper and mushrooms 5 minutes. Remove vegetables from pan; reserve. Blend flour and salt into oil remaining in pan; gradually add milk and salmon liquid; cook, stirring occasionally, until mixture thickens and comes to a boil. Beat egg yolks slightly; gradually add small amount of hot sauce; blend well, turn back into saucepan. Add salmon, green pepper, mushrooms and sour cream. Heat, but do not boil.

YIELD: *6 to 8 servings.*

OLD-FASHIONED MACARONI AND CHEESE

> 4 *cups cooked elbow macaroni*
> 2 *tablespoons butter or margarine*
> 1½ *cups shredded Cheddar cheese*
> 2 *eggs, beaten*
> 3 *cups milk*
> *Paprika*

Place macaroni in a 2½-quart casserole. Dot with butter and sprinkle with cheese. Combine eggs and milk; pour over macaroni. Sprinkle with paprika. Bake in 350° F. oven 40 minutes.

YIELD: *6 servings.*

RICOTTA EGG NOODLES

¼ cup butter or margarine
¼ pound ricotta cheese
2 eggs
½ teaspoon salt
2 cups sifted all-purpose flour

Cream butter until soft. Beat in ricotta and eggs. Blend well. Stir in salt and flour. Mix well. Roll paper-thin on floured board; cut into strips of any desired width. Let noodles dry thoroughly for several hours. Cook in boiling salted water for 10 minutes. Drain. Serve with butter, grated Parmesan cheese, and chopped parsley.

YIELD: *4 servings.*

SHELLFISH AND MACARONI CASSEROLE

2 cups broken macaroni
3 tablespoons butter or margarine
2 tablespoons minced onion
2 tablespoons flour
1½ cups milk
1 teaspoon salt
¼ teaspoon pepper
2 cups cut-up cooked lobster, shrimp, or crab meat
½ cup buttered bread crumbs
Paprika

Cook macaroni in boiling salted water according to package directions. Drain. Melt butter in saucepan; add onion and cook until tender but not brown. Blend in flour. Gradually add milk and cook, stirring constantly, until mixture thickens and comes to a boil. Add salt and pepper. Place layers of macaroni and shellfish in baking dish. Pour sauce over top. Sprinkle with crumbs and paprika. Bake in 350° F. oven 20 minutes.

YIELD: *6 servings.*

PASTINA WITH ZUCCHINI AND CLAMS

6 large clams
½ teaspoon salt
¼ teaspoon pepper
1 sprig parsley
1 thin slice garlic
2 cups sliced zucchini
½ cup pastina

Wash clams carefully. Place in saucepan with water. Heat until clams open up. Strain clam water through fine sieve and add enough water to make 2 cups. Place water in saucepan with salt, pepper, parsley, and garlic. Bring to a boil. Add zucchini. Simmer 2 minutes. Add pastina and simmer until tender, about 8 minutes. Remove clams from shell and chop very fine. Stir lightly into pastina mixture and serve immediately.

YIELD: *4 servings.*

PANCAKES, CRÊPES AND FRENCH TOAST

——◆——

SOUTHWESTERN ENCHILADA DINNER

3 cans (8 ounces each) tomato sauce
1½ teaspoons chili powder
1 cup milk
¾ cup cornstarch
⅓ cup white or yellow corn meal
½ teaspoon salt
2 eggs, beaten
2 tablespoons melted butter
2 cups shredded Cheddar cheese
1 cup chopped onion

Simmer tomato sauce and chili powder together, stirring occasionally, while making tortillas. For tortillas, mix milk and cornstarch to a smooth paste. Add with corn meal and salt to eggs. Stir in butter. For each tortilla, pour 3 tablespoons of the mixture into a buttered, heated 6-inch skillet. Brown on one side; turn and brown other side. Keep warm. For filling, combine cheese and onion. Dip tortillas, one at a time, in tomato sauce. Place 1 tortilla on buttered baking pan; sprinkle generous amount of cheese-onion mixture on it; repeat twice so as to have a stack of 3 layers. Make 3 more stacks. Heat in 350° F. oven, 10 minutes. If desired, top each stack with a fried egg sunny-side up. Pass remaining tomato sauce.

YIELD: *4 servings.*

SUPPER SPOON BREAD

1 can (11 ounces) condensed Cheddar cheese soup
½ soup can milk
½ cup corn meal
¼ cup butter or margarine
3 eggs, separated
½ teaspoon salt
¼ teaspoon baking powder

Stir soup until smooth in saucepan; gradually blend in milk.
Bring to boil, stirring occasionally. Reduce heat and gradually
add corn meal, stirring until just thickened. Remove from heat;
stir in butter. Beat egg yolks until thick; stir in a few tablespoons soup mixture. Blend yolks into remaining soup. Combine salt and baking powder; sprinkle over egg whites. Beat
until stiff, but not dry. Fold whites into the soup mixture. Turn
into a 1½-quart soufflé dish. Bake in a 350° F. oven 1 hour.

YIELD: *6 servings.*

PRONTO PIZZA

1 can (10¾ ounces) condensed tomato soup
1 small clove garlic, minced
4 English muffins, not sliced
Dried leaf oregano
Crushed red peppers, optional
4 ounces mozzarella or sharp Cheddar cheese, thinly
     sliced

Blend soup and garlic. Cut each muffin into 3 thin round
slices to form bases for pizzas; toast. Spread each with soup;
sprinkle with oregano and red peppers. Cut cheese into small
strips; place on top of sauce. Broil until cheese is melted.

YIELD: *12 small pizzas.*

ORANGE FRENCH TOAST

2 eggs, slightly beaten
3 tablespoons confectioners' sugar
1 teaspoon cinnamon
⅔ cup orange juice
2 teaspoons grated orange rind
10 slices bread
¼ cup butter or margarine
Honey, optional

Combine eggs, confectioners' sugar, cinnamon, orange juice, and orange rind. Dip bread slices into egg mixture, turning them to coat both sides. Brown bread, on both sides, in small amount of hot butter in a skillet. Serve with honey or confectioners' sugar.

YIELD: *5 servings.*

BUTTERMILK FRENCH TOAST

2 eggs, slightly beaten
1 cup buttermilk
⅛ teaspoon salt
12 slices whole wheat bread
¼ cup butter or margarine

Combine eggs, buttermilk, and salt. Dip bread slices into egg mixture, turning them to coat both sides. Brown bread, on both sides, in small amount of hot butter in a skillet. Serve with jelly, preserves, honey, or syrup.

YIELD: *6 servings.*

BANANA FRENCH TOAST

2 eggs, slightly beaten
⅔ cup milk
¼ teaspoon nutmeg
8 slices bread
¼ cup butter or margarine
3 medium bananas, sliced
Maple syrup

Combine eggs, milk, and nutmeg. Dip bread slices into egg mixture, turning them to coat both sides. Brown bread, on both sides, in small amount of hot butter in a skillet. Place a layer of sliced bananas on each of 4 slices of French toast.

Cover with a second slice of French toast. Serve with maple syrup.

YIELD: *4 servings.*

OVEN FRENCH TOAST

> *2 eggs, slightly beaten*
> *½ teaspoon salt*
> *2 tablespoons sugar*
> *1 cup milk*
> *½ teaspoon almond extract*
> *12 slices bread*

Combine eggs, salt, sugar, milk, and almond extract. Dip bread slices into mixture. Place slices on a well-greased cookie sheet and brown in a 450° F. oven about 10 minutes. Turn toast and continue browning. Serve with preserves, honey butter, or maple syrup.

YIELD: *6 servings.*

BUTTERSCOTCH PECAN TOAST

> *¼ cup soft butter or margarine*
> *½ cup brown sugar*
> *8 slices toast*
> *½ cup finely chopped pecans*

Combine butter and sugar. Spread each slice of toast with 1 tablespoon sugar mixture and sprinkle with 1 tablespoon pecans. Place toast, spread side up, on an ungreased cookie sheet. Toast under low broiler heat for 5 minutes. Serve immediately.

YIELD: *4 servings.*

PEANUT BUTTER FRENCH TOAST

¼ cup peanut butter
⅔ cup milk
2 eggs, slightly beaten
10 slices bread

Combine peanut butter and milk. Add eggs. Dip bread slices into mixture. Place slices on a well-greased cookie sheet and brown in a 450° F. oven about 10 minutes. Turn toast and continue browning. Serve with jelly, preserves, or honey.

YIELD: *5 servings.*

CRANBERRY FRENCH TOAST

2 eggs, slightly beaten
⅔ cup milk
⅛ teaspoon salt
1 teaspoon sugar
8 slices bread
¼ cup butter or margarine
4 slices jellied cranberry sauce, ¼ inch thick
Confectioners' sugar

Combine eggs, milk, salt, and sugar. Dip bread slices into egg mixture, turning them to coat both sides. Brown bread, on both sides, in small amount of hot butter in a skillet. Place a slice of jellied cranberry sauce between each 2 slices of French toast. Sprinkle with confectioners' sugar.

YIELD: *4 servings.*

APPLE CINNAMON TOAST

2 tablespoons soft butter or margarine
6 slices toast
2 tablespoons granulated sugar
1 teaspoon ground cinnamon
1½ cups applesauce

Spread 1 teaspoon butter on one side of each slice of toast. Combine sugar and cinnamon and sprinkle 1 teaspoon of mixture over buttered side of toast. Place toast, spread side up, on an ungreased cookie sheet. Toast in a 350° F. oven 5 minutes. Heat applesauce while toast is in oven. For each serving, spoon ½ cup applesauce on a slice of cinnamon toast. Cut a second slice of cinnamon toast in half diagonally and arrange over applesauce.

YIELD: *3 servings.*

ORANGE-CINNAMON FRENCH TOAST

1 can (6 ounces) frozen concentrated orange juice
2 eggs, beaten slightly
1 short loaf (1 pound) French bread
Butter
Cinnamon-sugar mixture

Cut frozen orange juice into small sections; add to beaten eggs in a shallow dish and blend together with a fork. Cut French bread into 16 equal-sized slices, each about 1 inch thick. Dip each slice into orange-egg mixture, turning to coat both sides. Fry until brown on both sides in a small amount of butter. Sprinkle each slice with cinnamon-sugar. Serve immediately.

YIELD: *8 servings.*

CALIFORNIA FRENCH TOAST

2 eggs, slightly beaten
½ teaspoon salt
2 tablespoons sugar
1 cup milk
½ teaspoon almond extract
12 slices bread
2 tablespoons confectioners' sugar
Slivered almonds

Combine beaten eggs, salt, sugar, milk, and almond extract in a shallow dish. Dip bread into egg mixture, 1 slice at a time, turn slices to coat both sides. Place dipped slices on a well-greased cookie sheet. Brown in a 450° F. oven 7 minutes. Turn toast and continue browning. Shake confectioners' sugar and slivered almonds over top of each slice. Serve immediately.

YIELD: *6 servings.*

STRAWBERRY TOASTWICH

¼ cup soft butter or margarine
12 slices bread
¾ cup strawberry preserves
2 eggs, slightly beaten
⅓ cup milk
½ teaspoon salt
1 tablespoon sugar
¼ cup butter or margarine
1½ tablespoons confectioners' sugar

Butter bread. Make 6 sandwiches by placing 2 tablespoons strawberry preserves between slices of buttered bread. Combine eggs, milk, salt, and sugar. Dip each sandwich into egg mixture, turning it to coat both sides. Brown sandwiches, on both sides, in small amount of hot butter in a skillet. Sift a little confectioners' sugar over top of each.

YIELD: *6 servings.*

TUNA SALAD-AMERICAN CHEESE
CLUB SANDWICH

1 can (6½ or 7 ounces) tuna, drained and flaked
½ cup chopped stuffed olives
⅓ cup mayonnaise or salad dressing
½ cup soft butter or margarine
16 slices white bread toast
8 slices whole wheat bread toast
8 lettuce leaves
8 thick slices American cheese

Combine tuna, olives, and mayonnaise. Butter toast. Cover each of 8 slices of buttered white toast with a lettuce leaf, tuna salad, and a slice of whole wheat toast. Top each sandwich with a cheese slice and finish with a slice of buttered white toast.

YIELD: *8 servings.*

FRENCH-TOASTED SALMON SANDWICHES

1 can (8 ounces) salmon, drained and flaked
½ cup finely chopped celery
2 tablespoons chopped green pepper
1 tablespoon minced onion
¼ teaspoon salt
Dash pepper
4 tablespoons mayonnaise or salad dressing
8 slices bread

1 egg, slightly beaten
½ cup milk
Butter or margarine

Combine salmon with celery, green pepper, onion, salt, pepper, and mayonnaise. Spread salmon mixture over 4 slices of bread; top with remaining bread. Dip sandwiches in mixture of egg and milk. Fry until golden brown on both sides in small amount of butter. Serve piping hot.

YIELD: *4 servings.*

SHRIMP-CRAB BISQUE SANDWICHES

1 can (10½ ounces) condensed cream of shrimp soup
1 can (7¾ ounces) crab meat
2 tablespoons minced celery
2 tablespoons minced green pepper
1 tablespoon minced onion
2 tablespoons mayonnaise
Few drops lemon juice
¼ teaspoon Worcestershire sauce
Salt
Pepper
4 slices toast or rusks
Grated Parmesan cheese
⅓ cup milk

Measure out ¼ cup soup; mix with crab meat, celery, green pepper, onion, mayonnaise, lemon juice, and seasonings. Place toast or rusks on cookie sheet. Top with crab mixture. Sprinkle with cheese. Bake in 425° F. oven 10 to 15 minutes or until hot. Combine remaining soup with milk in saucepan. Heat to serving temperature. Serve as sauce over sandwiches.

YIELD: *4 servings.*

COTTAGE BLINTZES

1 egg
1 cup milk
1 cup sifted all-purpose flour
½ teaspoon salt
¼ cup butter, melted
1 cup cottage cheese
2 tablespoons butter, softened
1 egg
1 cup sour cream

Beat egg, milk, flour, and salt together to mix thoroughly. Pour ½ tablespoon butter into 6-inch skillet; add ¼ cup batter to cover bottom of pan. Cook over low heat until the one side is set. Lift blintz from pan onto clean cloth, browned side up; cool. Repeat. Batter will make 8 blintzes. Make filling by beating together cottage cheese, butter, and egg; spread each blintz thickly with this mixture and roll. Place lapped side down on buttered baking sheet. Bake in 350° F. oven 20 minutes. Top blintzes with sour cream.

SPICY APPLESAUCE WITH CHEESE-FILLED PANCAKES

SAUCE:

1 can (1 pound) applesauce
1 tablespoon butter
½ teaspoon nutmeg
½ teaspoon ground cinnamon

Combine applesauce, butter, nutmeg, and cinnamon in saucepan and simmer 5 minutes. Serve over pancakes.

FILLING AND PANCAKES:

¾ pound cottage cheese
1 egg yolk

1½ teaspoons sugar
½ teaspoon ground cinnamon
2 eggs
½ cup milk
½ cup sifted all-purpose flour
½ teaspoon salt
Butter

Press cheese through sieve; add egg yolk, beating well. Add sugar and cinnamon; mix well and reserve to fill pancakes. Beat eggs, add milk. Gradually add liquid to flour and salt, beating until smooth. Heat 6-inch skillet; grease with butter. Pour enough batter, about 2 tablespoons, into skillet to make a very thin pancake, tipping skillet from side to side to cover bottom. Fry on both sides. After pancakes are made, place rounded tablespoon of cheese mixture in center of each and fold. Serve with hot spicy applesauce.

YIELD: *4 servings.*

APPLE FLAPJACK

1¼ cups sifted all-purpose flour
2½ teaspoons baking powder
3 tablespoons sugar
¾ teaspoon salt
¼ teaspoon ground cinnamon
2 eggs, separated
1 cup milk
3 tablespoons salad oil
1 cup finely grated peeled apples

Sift flour with baking powder, sugar, salt, and cinnamon. Beat egg yolks, add milk and oil. Slowly add liquid to dry ingredients. Beat until batter is smooth. Add grated apples and fold in stiffly beaten egg whites. Drop by tablespoonfuls on greased skillet, spreading each cake out lightly with back of spoon. Cook on one side until puffed, bubbly, and browned on edge. Turn and cook other side.

YIELD: *4 servings.*

COTTAGE CHEESE PANCAKES

3 eggs, well beaten
1 cup creamed cottage cheese
2 tablespoons melted butter or margarine
¼ cup sifted all-purpose flour
¼ teaspoon salt
Butter
Jelly

Combine all ingredients and mix well until blended. Fry until golden brown on both sides in a small amount of butter. Serve with butter or spread with favorite jelly.

YIELD: *4 servings.*

CHINESE SHRIMP PANCAKES

8 pancakes
¼ cup sliced water chestnuts
2 tablespoons thinly sliced scallions
2 tablespoons butter or margarine
1 can (10½ ounces) condensed cream of shrimp soup
1 cup diced cooked shrimp
¼ teaspoon soy sauce
2 tablespoons milk
¼ teaspoon Worcestershire sauce
⅛ teaspoon Tabasco

Prepare pancakes; keep warm. Cook water chestnuts and scallions in butter 5 minutes. Add ¼ cup of soup, shrimp, and soy sauce. Place 2 tablespoons of filling on each pancake; roll. Keep warm in oven. Combine remaining soup, milk, Worcestershire sauce, and Tabasco in saucepan. Heat to serving temperature. Serve as sauce over pancakes.

YIELD: *4 servings.*

CORN PANCAKES

1 cup evaporated milk
1 cup water
2 cups packaged pancake mix
1 cup drained whole-kernel corn

Mix together milk and water. Blend in pancake mix; stir in corn. Use about 3 tablespoons of batter for each pancake, and bake on oiled skillet or griddle. Turn only once. Keep warm.

YIELD: *5 servings.*

APPLE PANCAKES

1 egg
1 tablespoon sugar
1 tablespoon softened butter
1 medium apple, pared, cored, and quartered
1 cup evaporated milk
1 cup packaged pancake mix

Place egg, sugar, butter, apple, and evaporated milk in container of electric blender. Cover and run at low speed for a few seconds until apple is chopped. Add pancake mix. Cover and run at high speed a few seconds longer until blended. Pour about ¼ cup at a time in oiled skillet or griddle. Bake until bubbles appear on top and underside is browned, turn and bake to brown second side. Keep warm. Serve hot with Cinnamon Syrup (below).

YIELD: *4 servings.*

CINNAMON SYRUP

1 cup light corn syrup
2 cups sugar
½ cup water
2 teaspoons ground cinnamon
1 cup evaporated milk

Combine corn syrup, sugar, water, and cinnamon in a saucepan. Bring to a full boil over medium heat, stirring constantly. Continue stirring and boiling for an additional 2 minutes. Cool 5 minutes; then stir in evaporated milk. Serve warm over Apple Pancakes.

CREAMED LOBSTER WITH ALMONDS OVER PANCAKES

8 pancakes
1 cup chopped celery
2 tablespoons butter or margarine
1 can (10¾ ounces) condensed cream of chicken or
    mushroom soup
⅓ to ½ cup milk
1 cup diced cooked lobster
2 tablespoons diced pimiento
¼ cup toasted slivered almonds

Prepare pancakes; keep warm. Cook celery in butter in saucepan until tender; blend in soup and milk. Add lobster, pimiento, and almonds. Heat to serving temperature. Serve over pancakes.

YIELD: *4 servings.*

RICE PANCAKES

2 cups sifted all-purpose flour
2 teaspoons baking powder
1 teaspoon salt
2 tablespoons sugar
4 eggs, separated
5 tablespoons shortening
2 cups milk
1½ cups cold cooked rice

Sift together dry ingredients into a mixing bowl. Beat egg whites and yolks separately. Combine egg yolks, shortening, and milk. Add to the dry ingredients. Mix well. Stir in rice. Fold in stiffly beaten egg whites. Bake on hot griddle.

YIELD: *4 servings.*

SHRIMP-FILLED CRÊPES

1¾ cups milk, divided
1 can (10½ ounces) condensed cream of shrimp soup
2 eggs, slightly beaten
3 tablespoons melted shortening
¾ cup buttermilk pancake mix
1 can (4½ ounces) shrimp

Combine ½ cup milk and cream of shrimp soup in saucepan. Heat and keep warm. Combine eggs, remaining 1¼ cups milk, shortening, and pancake mix. Beat until smooth. Pour scant ¼ cup batter in oiled skillet or griddle. Bake until underside is browned, turn and bake other side. Place several shrimp in center; roll. Place rolled crêpes side by side in greased baking dish. Cover with sauce. Heat in 350° F. oven 10 to 15 minutes.

YIELD: *3 servings.*

DOWN EAST CRÊPES

1 can (10¾ ounces) condensed cream of mushroom soup
½ cup milk
3 eggs
3 tablespoons salad oil, divided
1 can (7¾ ounces) crab meat, flaked
1 tablespoon chopped parsley
¾ teaspoon salt, divided
¼ teaspoon dried leaf oregano
⅔ cup milk
½ cup sifted all-purpose flour

Combine soup and ½ cup milk in saucepan and heat. Set aside. Beat 1 egg slightly. Add 1 tablespoon oil, crab meat, parsley, ¼ teaspoon salt, and oregano; mix well. Set aside. In a medium bowl beat remaining 2 eggs, ⅔ cup milk, and remaining 2 tablespoons oil until smooth. Add flour and remaining ½ teaspoon salt; mix until smooth. Place batter, 2 tablespoons at a time, on hot griddle; brown for 1 minute; turn and brown other side. Place generous spoonful of filling on each crêpe. Roll up and place in shallow 2-quart baking dish. Pour sauce over crêpes. Bake in 350° F. oven 20 minutes.

YIELD: *4 servings.*

VEGETABLE CRÊPES

CRÊPES:

1 cup milk
¼ cup water
3 eggs
1 cup whole wheat flour

¼ *cup wheat germ*
3 *tablespoons salad oil*
½ *teaspoon salt*
⅛ *teaspoon Tabasco*

FILLING:

1 *bunch broccoli*
1½ *teaspoons salt, divided*
1 *tablespoon salad oil*
¼ *cup chopped onion*
1 *tomato, peeled and diced*
¼ *teaspoon dried leaf marjoram*
¼ *teaspoon Tabasco*
1½ *cups shredded Cheddar cheese, divided*
2 *tablespoons butter*

To make crêpes: Combine all crêpe ingredients in container of electric blender. Cover and process until smooth. Chill 1 hour. Lightly grease the surface of an 8-inch skillet or crêpe pan. Place over medium heat until very hot. Pour 3 tablespoons batter in center of pan and tilt pan in all directions until bottom is coated with batter. Pour any excess batter back into uncooked batter. Cook until crêpe begins to pull away from sides of pan and is lightly browned. Turn and cook briefly on other side, about 30 seconds. Continue until all batter is used.

To make filling: Trim leaves and bottom of stem from broccoli and chop remaining stems and buds. Place in skillet with ½ teaspoon salt and water to a depth of ¼ inch. Bring to boil, cover, reduce heat, and cook until crisp-tender, about 10 minutes. Drain. Heat oil in skillet. Add onion and cook until tender. Remove from heat; stir in tomato, cooked broccoli, remaining 1 teaspoon salt, marjoram, Tabasco, and 1 cup shredded Cheddar cheese. Place 1 tablespoon filling down center of each crêpe and roll up crêpe. Place seam side down in greased baking dish. Sprinkle with remaining ½ cup cheese and dot with butter. Bake in 400° F. oven until thoroughly heated, about 15 minutes.

YIELD: *16 crêpes; 8 servings.*

INDEX